MW00399174

THE SHATTERING

The names of all individuals mentioned in this book, except the author, her husband,
and the couple from the Living Ranch, have been changed to protect their identity.

Address all personal correspondence to:
Jessica Smith
Email: *Jess.ahner.smith@gmail.com*
Website: *www.truthbehindyoga.com*

Individuals and groups may order books from the author directly, or from the
publisher. Retailers and wholesalers should order from our distributors. Refer to the
Deeper Revelation Books website for distribution information, as well as an online
catalog of all our books.

Published by:
Deeper Revelation Books
Revealing "the deep things of God" (1 Cor. 2:10)
P.O. Box 4260
Cleveland, TN 37320
423-478-2843
Website: *www.deeperrevelationbooks.org*
Email: *info@deeperrevelationbooks.org*

Deeper Revelation Books assists Christian authors in publishing and distributing
their books. Final responsibility for design, content, veracity and factuality of stories
and statements, permissions, editorial accuracy, and doctrinal views, either expressed
or implied, belongs to the author.

Dedication

This book is dedicated to truth, and to those who seek it. And to my mom, who for so many years never stopped praying for its revealing in my life.

ာ ာ ာ

Acknowledgments

I would like to thank all of you who contributed to make this book a reality—you know who you are. Your encouragement, feedback and generosity are appreciated beyond measure.

I would also like to specifically thank my husband for being so amazingly supportive. Your heart amazes me daily.

Contents

Part 1:
My Story

Introduction

The story I'm about to share is so dramatic you might be tempted to write it off as fantasy. It reads like a novel, but it's real life—my life. If I were testifying on the witness stand instead of in these pages, I would raise my right hand and take the oath, solemnly swearing that what I'm about to share is the whole truth, and nothing but the truth, so help me God.

In some ways my story is not so unusual. After rebelling from my Christian upbringing, I spent my twenties traveling the world and exploring the spiritual realm of meditative practices in an effort to find real truth and peace. My ultimate goal was a good one: to make the world a better place by sharing what I learned along the way. Like many on this path, I thought the Bible was ridiculous and Christians were arrogant bigots (with extremely obnoxious tastes in music). It got to the point that I cringed at the name of Jesus, so irritated was I by his followers, and grew to use his name solely as a swear word.

At some point, I decided to get all the negativity out of my life—including my disapproving sentiments toward Jesus. I felt badly about being disrespectful to such a great teacher and healer. I never would have used Buddha's name as a curse word. And, really, it was Jesus' followers who must have corrupted his teachings. How could I blame him for that?

So one night, I asked Jesus to forgive me. Then I decided to go a step further: because my practices were all focused around energy healing, and because Jesus was said to be the master healer, I asked him to work with me. I would try to follow his path—not the path of the typical (judgmental) Christian. I was done with that. I wanted to know what Jesus had to say—not some guy with a tie and a Bible to thump.

Never could I have fathomed where this new path would lead me. How could I have imagined, outside of fiction, that a terrifying spiritual experience would shatter my entire life paradigm? How could I possibly accept what I long believed to be an impossibility: that the very real spiritual world we live in is saturated with deception in which darkness masks itself as light disguised in visions, esoteric experiences, and even feelings, sensations, and moments of supposed inspiration?

If you had handed me this book before these events happened, I would likely have stopped reading the first time Jesus' name was mentioned. You might feel the same way. But I earnestly ask you to please set aside any preconceived notions of anything religious, and just hear my story for what it is: a truthful account of a spiritual journey so intensely personal and revealing that, were it not for the urgency pressing from the depths of my being, I swear I would tuck the whole thing away and never say a word about it.

But doing that would be like running out of a burning house without bothering to yell, "Fire!" to anyone inside. So I am yelling. Please, at least hear the words. Then decide if you want to stay in the house.

1
AND SO IT BEGINS...

I grew up in a Christian home—well, half-Christian, anyway. From my earliest memory (and likely before that), my mom raised me in the faith. My dad would go to church on holidays and rare occasions in an attempt to appease my mom, and perhaps to search for something more. But she was the one who taught me to pray to God through Jesus. She explained that God was Jesus and Jesus was God.

From my mom I learned that God came to earth through Jesus. He came to save us from our sins because that was God's plan, and he was our Father. Because I was a kid and I believed my mom, I didn't feel the need to know or ask *why*. I loved the idea of having a dad in heaven. And I loved praying; I talked to God all the time and trusted wholeheartedly that he heard me. I remember going upstairs to my room to read my Bible and pray.

I'm not trying to paint a picture of me as the perfect child— far from it. I made my sister play with the old Barbies while I took the new ones, threw fits when I didn't get what I wanted, and licked the last donut so my brothers wouldn't eat it. I could be a real brat. But I still loved to pray and talk to Jesus.

As I grew up, being popular became increasingly important to me. I had lots of insecurities, and I thought being accepted by my peers would alleviate them. It wasn't enough to be accepted by the Christian kids because they weren't cool, and I didn't feel like I connected with any of them anyway. What I wanted was to be popular with a larger group and for boys to like me.

Then, in my sophomore year of high school, I made the dance team and my wish came true. The transition was quick once I was on the team. All the popular girls I hoped would talk to me started inviting me to hang out with them. Soon I was smoking, drinking, and trying pot. That's what these girls did, and they seemed to be having lots of fun. Everyone knew who they were; all the boys liked them; all the girls were jealous of them; and everyone wanted to hang out with them because they were just . . . cool.

It made me feel grown-up to do what I wasn't supposed to do. I could make my own decisions, and there wasn't a single thing my parents could do about it. It felt good to rebel against what was expected of me. I was the "token Christian" of the group, but this high school period was when I started questioning everything about Christianity that didn't make sense to me. I was not satisfied with being told to "just have faith." It started to sound like an excuse Christians used to answer difficult questions.

So I prayed less and rebelled more. At the end of high school, I was pretty torn between the way I knew I should be living and the way I was living. Part of me felt badly for being such a rebellious brat. So I gave in to my mom's desire for me to attend a private Christian college, figuring I would give God another go.

The Christian college was much stricter than I had thought it would be. They wanted me to go to church three times a week. Boys weren't even allowed in my dorm room. I had a curfew earlier than the one I had at home. The students played Bible Trivia and had prayer circles on Saturday night. None of this seemed like a fit for me. I just wanted to hang out with cute boys and drink beer. In my eyes, the students' happiness was so fake that it repulsed me. I wondered how anyone could be happy spending a Saturday night like that.

From the moment I arrived on campus, I felt rebellion rising within me, and I embraced it. My first assignment in speech class was a "how-to" presentation that required a physical prop and taught a moral lesson. One guy brought in some baseball object—a bat or glove or something—and taught us all how to swing or catch or perform some other fundamental baseball skill. I think his lesson was about the importance of not giving up. A girl brought in a patchwork quilt she and her grandma had made together. She explained the process of quilting, weaving in wisdom and life lessons from her elders.

I decided to take my speech in a different direction. I walked up with no obvious prop other than a sheet of folded notebook paper with my scribbled but organized notes. I explained how some of my friends went from being star athletes to drug addicts, and I showed how easy it was to hide addictions. I began pulling my "hidden" props out of my pocket—a plastic sandwich bag filled with baking soda, my bank card, a cosmetic compact with a mirror—and taught the class how to chop, line up, and snort lines of cocaine or meth (I'd called a friend the night before to ask about the process).

I reveled in the shocked expression on my professor's face and proceeded to befriend the only other rebels at school: one guy who was sent there as punishment, and another guy in a situation similar to mine. We left campus to drink beer and smoke as many cigarettes as possible.

After completing the last final exam of my first semester, I promptly packed my belongings and transferred to a non-Christian school.

Knowing God and the true nature of all things spiritual had been important to me for as long as I could remember. I had a very real sense that forever was so much longer than our short lives. I wanted to know more about *forever* than about the short blip called *life*; and I wanted to know how this life affects what comes after.

For example, what was our purpose for being here in the big scheme of eternity? I sometimes questioned the Bible and wondered if there was anything more to "truth" than what was in there. The Bible didn't seem to answer all my questions clearly, which really frustrated me. I felt like I deserved to have answers. What about the people in remote villages who had never heard about Jesus? Why do bad things happen if God is loving and in charge of everything?

And So It Begins... 15

Every time a conversation with another Christian went in this direction, they mentioned faith in their reply. The term started to sound more like an excuse for dead-ends, roadblocks, unclear or tough issues, and unanswered questions. I was deeply dissatisfied with their answers, especially during my stint at the Christian college. Everyone seemed so phony. I felt judged by them because I didn't raise my hands during the singing in chapel and didn't join their prayer circles or play Bible Trivia on the weekends.

In reality, a lot of the judgment I felt was probably self-judgment that I projected onto them. Wherever it came from, I felt judged, and it only made me want to rebel even more against everything my classmates stood for. So I decided that what they called *faith* was a cop-out—the positive connotative equivalent of its negative counterpart: *naïveté*.

I really didn't know what I believed anymore. I simply knew I didn't want to be like anyone at that Christian college. Although I still had an underlying belief in God and the Bible, I was sick of thinking about it and tired of trying to figure out what I believed. So after transferring schools, I pushed the whole subject of religion and spirituality out of mind. I stopped going to church almost completely and focused on doing my schoolwork, working to pay for school, and filling any in-between time with partying, drinking, and experimenting with drugs I had always been dead-set against. Somehow, the fact that my gorgeous, soccer-star boyfriend was doing it made the disgusting idea much more attractive.

2
CHANGING SIDES

After a couple years of continued spiritual indifference, something happened that forced me to confront what I believed: a friend was killed in a drunk-driving accident. I was desperate to know what happened to her. My mind raced with possibilities. None of them brought comfort because I just didn't know where her spirit was.

My friend had been fun, sweet, and beautiful. Everyone loved her. She was the girl who was popular, yet still nice to everyone. I wasn't sure if she was a Christian, though. According to what I had been taught my entire life, there was a possibility she was in a place called *hell*.

I was unwilling to consider such a prospect, because the Bible says God both created us and loves us. If that was true, how could there even be a chance he would allow my sweet friend to go to hell? For days I cried in desperate confusion regarding her whereabouts and became angry toward the whole Christianity thing for causing me such upheaval. I just wanted to know where my friend was. After days of turmoil, I had this weird feeling that I should call a certain relative. The thought was strange because at that point, I barely knew this person. We had seen each other only a couple times when I was younger. The extent of our relationship after that was our short, twice-yearly phone calls during which I would thank her for the great birthday and Christmas presents she had sent me.

I was so upset about my friend's death that I didn't even feel like talking to people I knew well and was comfortable around. I wondered why I had the thought of calling this person for help. I tried disregarding the idea, but it persisted until finally, at a total loss, I gave in. I got her number from my mom, shut myself in her bedroom, and dialed.

A soft, sweet voice answered. At the sound of it, desperate, pleading tears flowed instantly from my eyes. "Hi," I began, "it's Jessica. I...I...," I stammered, searching for words that would make sense. But none came.

"I don't know why I'm calling you." I paused again in scrambled thought while she waited patiently. "My friend just died...and I...." Why was I even calling? I could not find words.

"I just want to know where she is!" I finally blurted, and broke into sobs.

The calm and comforting voice soothed me immediately. "Honey, what is your friend's name—her full name?"

"Lela—er, Lela Walker. I don't know her middle name."

"That's okay," the loving voice continued. "Honey, Lela wants you to know that she is okay. She is here with me now. Do you have anything you want to ask her?"

As my relative spoke, something strange started happening to me. I can best describe it as a rushing wave—an intense, euphoric, warm, "energy" (for lack of a better word) that began in the bottoms of my feet and shot through my whole body in blissful peace. But it was not just a *feeling* of peace; it was a literal, physical sensation that exceeded the limits of human vocabulary. It would be like trying to explain a color to someone who has never experienced eyesight. I had certainly never felt anything like it before.

This energy seemed like a miracle to me. Although I had never entertained the idea that psychics or communicating with spirits or anything of the sort was even a possibility (I knew the Bible strictly warned against it), this physical energy was so intensely peaceful that it immediately validated the thought that what my relative was telling me must be true. After all, I had been praying to God for answers, and God is love. Now, what felt like the essence of pure love was shooting through my being and flooding me in euphoric waves.

On the phone in my mom's room, as my entire being surged with this serene energy, I was overwhelmed by the seeming

THE SHATTERING

goodness and legitimacy of the experience. Here I was, thinking I had the opportunity to talk to my sweet friend who had just passed into another mysterious realm of existence. My mind overflowed with humble gratitude for such an incredibly amazing opportunity. I wanted to know everything!

But what does one *ask* in such a moment? The phone line went silent as my brain whirled. Finally, I blurted out the first thing that came to mind.

"Did it hurt when you died?"

My relative's voice replied. "No. I remember getting on the motorcycle. I knew I shouldn't have. I knew it was stupid. Something just made me do it. And we were going way too fast around the corner. I remember flying off and hitting something really hard, but there wasn't any pain."

She moved on quickly from the scene. "And then Jess, I was in this place where I am now. And…oh, this place is… incredible. I can't even begin to explain how amazing it is. But Jess, just know it's amazing!"

My relative lived a significant distance away from me. The accident had happened far from both of us. So she definitely had not seen any news regarding Lela's death. Even if she had, she would have been completely unaware that I knew her. No one had called to inform her that I had a friend who passed away. Yet here she was telling me the details of a motorcycle accident. Any shred of doubt about the legitimacy of this miraculous event was extinguished. I was convinced that I was having a conversation with my friend.

Throughout the conversation she told me many things through what I assumed was Lela's spirit talking. The exchange was always in my relative's voice, but the manner in which she spoke sometimes even mimicked Lela's style. She told me details about reincarnation and why she had to die when she did so that she could fulfill her purpose in the next life. She divulged other things that seemed to reveal secrets about the spiritual world and what the afterlife was like—things the Bible had never told me. I was so grateful for the new knowledge I had been given. The strange, peaceful energy, the details she knew—this thing had to be real; it *felt* so real. Before the phone call, I never would have thought about consulting someone who claimed to communicate with spirits. By the time I hung up, I had a brand-new paradigm and was convinced of a new reality—a reality of spirits and reincarnation and unbelievably peaceful, loving energy. I sat on the edge of the bed completely calm, still buzzing from the energy's residue, overjoyed with what I viewed as the outstanding gift I had just received. My mind grabbed hold of it, trying to process all that had happened.

At the same time, I still wanted to believe the Bible, and felt a strange, deep guilt for questioning it. Wanting that feeling to go away, I started looking into what the Bible said about reincarnation, hoping to find a loophole to justify what I wanted to believe.

I found a verse that said "People are destined to die once, and after that to face judgment."[1] I was disappointed because it stated pretty clearly that we die only once. Relentless in my desire to make the Bible fit what I wanted it to say, I reasoned that maybe the soul is what dies once, after living many lives. So I settled the reincarnation issue for myself and decided not to give it any more thought. But there was one remaining issue with which I struggled. I knew the Bible strictly, repeatedly, and adamantly warned against communicating with the dead. (If you're curious, you can find some of these references in Chapter 21.)

The whole idea of spirits had always creeped me out a bit. So I liked to think that the admonition against communicating with them was given because spirits weren't real anyway. If I had opened my eyes to the verses, I would have seen that the Bible clearly teaches otherwise. In any event, at that point I chose to believe in the existence of spirits because I knew my relative was full of love and wasn't just pulling a fast one on me.

As much as I tried to rationalize it away, I could not fully shake the nagging sense that the only biblical explanation for the experience was that my relative and I were being deceived by evil spirits pretending to be Lela. I might even have entertained this idea were it not for the energy shooting so beautifully through my body like blood coursing through my physical veins. There was no way, I thought, that an evil spirit could ever be accompanied by such feelings of peace and love—especially when I had desperately prayed to God for the truth. Would he let me be led astray like that?

My decision here was crucial. I had the chance to believe what I knew the Bible said, even though I didn't understand and didn't want to believe it. It was my choice.

But I didn't even know whether I believed in evil spirits. It seemed possible to me that as translations of the Bible were developed, people added the stuff about demons so more people could be won to religion through fear.

That's where the slippery slope of my next ten years began: I decided that *parts* of the Bible (namely, the parts that didn't suit my desired perspective), must have been changed or mistranslated. It was a difficult position to justify, knowing that the Bible forbade communicating with spirits. But I finally brushed aside the issue and decided that throughout the years, people in power had added these parts to suit their own agendas.

Eventually, the gnawing unease and guilt went away.

Thus began my newfound hunger for anything "spiritual," which I then viewed as the real truth. The intense energy of peace and love I had experienced while speaking to my relative was incredible. Never had I experienced anything as "spiritual" or profound while praying to Jesus. In all my years of praying to him, I never felt physical, euphoric energy shooting through my body.

I wanted to know how to have that feeling and experience again. I also wanted to learn to help people the way I believed my relative had so tremendously helped me: I wanted to know how I, too, could communicate with spirits.

Changing Sides

3
GROWTH OF THE SPIRITUAL

I soon discovered a new section of the bookstore called *Metaphysics/New Age*. I wondered how I had never allowed myself to be interested in this stuff before. An entire world of possibilities opened up to me. It was as though my eyes had finally been opened to the truth of how things really were—the truth I'd been praying for ever since religious doubts first crept into my youthful mind. Finally, my prayers had paid off and it was being revealed.

I begged my relative for instruction, and she introduced me to meditation. Trying to focus my constant thoughts on one thing was frustrating, but I found that the more I practiced, the more peaceful I felt. I was taught that meditation was the key to my development on this spiritual path. If I wanted to communicate with spirits as my relative did, see the things she saw, and help people the way she helped me when Lela died, I would have to practice and develop these skills.

The next nine years of my life were dedicated, more or less, to this spiritual path. The *less* part was due only to the constant distractions of fun and adventure. But no matter how distracted I was by play and parties, I always tried to infuse my meditation practices into life, sometimes meditating through hangovers on beaches in Central and South America. I would also travel to study meditative traditions and take long sabbaticals at retreat centers to deepen my practices and refocus.

My spiritual growth was always on my mind, and constantly evolving.

ço ço ço

I began my meditation practice with the common beginner's instruction to "focus on the breath." Oh, it was frustrating! Often I would finish meditation more bothered than when I started! But every once in a while, for a few moments, I would feel a certain stillness and peace and be inspired to continue. With practice, I would occasionally feel a subtle version of the same peaceful energy I had felt during my initial experience after my friend died; but it was never anywhere close to being as strong.

Soon I learned that meditation simply meant to focus on one thing so thoughts would lessen and cease and my mind could become quiet and reach a state of "openness." The breath didn't have to be my only focus. In fact, there were infinite ways of quieting and opening the mind. I was taught that we could even focus on, pay reverence to, and invoke the spirits of Jesus, Mother Teresa, and other Christian saints by using mental or physical pictures of them. The idea of opening this way really appealed to me; I loved a spiritual approach that seemed all-inclusive and nonjudgmental, able to love and respect all religions.

I discovered that the practice of quieting one's thoughts led to more than an experience of overwhelming peace. It also opened one to the spiritual realm. I was taught that praying is talking to God, and meditating is listening.

This can be confusing because the term *meditation* has two opposing definitions. This is not widely known in our culture, so the terms are often confused and used interchangeably. I explain the differences at some length in Chapter 22; but it's important to mention them briefly here. The two definitions are: (1) the biblical definition and, (2) the Eastern spiritual definition, often called "mindfulness" meditation. The biblical definition basically means "to think about." The practice of mindfulness meditation is exactly the opposite: it means to let go of thought and empty the mind (typically by focusing on a single object such as the breath)—thereby opening it to (and inviting in) the spiritual realm. Mindfulness meditation is increasingly presented on talk shows, in magazines, and even proposed in public-school curricula as a non-spiritual, scientific practice, but this is far from the case. Understanding this is really important, so I strongly urge you to read Chapters 22 and 23 upon completion of this story (it will make more sense). For now, however, the only form of meditation I will be discussing is according to the Eastern or mindfulness definition, not the biblical one.

Mindfulness meditation is training *to become open to the spiritual realm*. Any "relaxation" technique of meditation is a baby step taken at the beginning stages of this discipline. I was taught that in order to communicate with "God," deities, spirits, guides, or energies (i.e., to tap into the spiritual world as a listener and receiver of information), it was critical to develop in the mind the state of openness meditation produced.

Because of how peaceful and full of love I felt when practicing meditation, I never doubted that it was the right path. The more regularly I meditated, the more love, peace, calm, and patience I seemed to sense in my daily life. My path was also validated by the increased depth and esoteric nature of my experiences both within and outside of my meditation practices. These factors convinced me that I was progressing in truth along my spiritual path.

One winter, while living in Berkeley, California, I began attending weekly spiritual development and meditation classes in Palo Alto. With traffic, the drive took an hour each way. The experiences I had in the sessions were so powerful (much more intense than my meditation practice on my own) that I would have driven much greater distances to attend. I was cheerfully addicted to this peaceful energy, and driving an hour each way was a small price for my weekly "fix."

Another winter found me living at a Buddhist center so I could focus completely on cultivating my meditation practice. My practice deepened as I developed stronger skills and a calmer, more peaceful state of overall being—all while working with Buddhist deities. Never had I been happier or more filled with peaceful love than when I was living at the Buddhist center. I thought surely this was indicative of being on the

Growth of the Spiritual

spiritual path of truth.

In addition to a more peaceful mind, I experienced more frequent and stronger versions of the initial flow of physical energy I felt during my very first encounter after Lela passed away. I learned about my "energy body" and discovered how to manipulate, control, and direct the flow of energy for healing. I began reiki training, an energy healing practice that channels spiritual energies into the practitioner's body and out through the hands for purposes of healing. I was drawn to deepen my practice and drawn to the place where my meditation practices originated. Wanting to learn from the purest of teachers, I began research and purchased tickets to Delhi, India.

4
GOING DEEPER IN INDIA

I traveled to India for no purpose other than spiritual growth—to learn and grow so that I could come home more prepared to share with others the lessons of truth, peace, healing, and love. Well, and there was probably a bit of traveler's pride mixed in there, too. Many of my co-adventuring, travel-addict friends claimed that on multiple levels, India was among the most challenging countries to explore. If you could travel India, you could do anything.

I wanted to do it, and I wanted to do it solo. My long-term goal was to begin working on plans to open a center of meditation, yoga, and reiki upon my return. Dates lined up perfectly for me to attend an annual Tibetan Buddhist event in Northern India (sponsored by the Buddhist center where I had lived), and then travel to a yoga teacher-training program under a very respected and traditional Indian teacher.

My introduction to yoga had occurred years prior. My first couple of trips to the yoga class at the gym left me wondering why people bothered with it. I did not see what all the hype was about. I felt like it was going nowhere; I was neither meditating nor getting a workout. Then I happened upon a class in Central America that left me feeling both meditatively peaceful and physically spent. *I was hooked.*

Having sampled the real thing, I felt there was a spiritual depth to yoga that was being lost in the Westernized version presented in gym classes. I wanted to explore yoga's origins and learn about its spiritual foundation. Then I would be able to deepen my own practice and help preserve the tradition. I wanted to share the benefits I believed came from tapping into the root of the spiritual practice, instead of just going through the poses for the sake of a workout.

Yoga also seemed to be an excellent tool in introducing

people to the benefits of meditation, especially as it was becoming so popularized in Western nations. Of course, I had mixed feelings about the Westernization of yoga: On one hand, I believed yoga was being diluted as classes became more focused on fitness. On the other hand, using a gym class to market the spiritual practice of yoga was genius!

What better way to get a body-obsessed culture interested in a spiritual practice than to focus on its physical benefits? It was brilliant to repackage the ancient spiritual practice as a trendy, sexy, body-sculpting class. At least people would attend! And it would open a crack into the spiritual world, drawing people who would otherwise reject Eastern spirituality or religions.

My thought was that even those prone to scoffing at the idea of meditation or spirituality would gradually become more accepting of both. People would come for the physical benefits, but hopefully get interested in the unexpected "side effects" of peacefulness. That would make the practice of meditation more inviting, too.

But before I could pursue the vision, I needed to train where I would learn the true roots of the practice, not some telephone-game, Westernized version.

After spending time deepening my meditation practice at sacred Buddhist sites in Northeast India, I traveled to an ashram[2] to start yoga teacher training. I liked the teacher immediately. He was an Indian man of small stature who exuded a humble kindness, and his eyes had a fatherly, nurturing spark that ignited in me excitement at the prospect of discovering the knowledge behind them. The yogi had left his home in India as a young child to live and study at an ashram where his uncle, a revered yogi, resided. He had been studying and practicing ever since—almost his entire lifetime.

The program focused on the whole, traditional approach to

yoga. It taught everything I wanted to know about the reality of the practice. I had heard it said that *yoga* means to "yoke." It is often explained in our culture that this means to yoke together body and mind, but I discovered that the real meaning of *yoke* goes deeper— yoking oneself with an esoteric idea of a universal godhead, the supposed source of all knowledge and creation.

The ancient religious doctrine of yoga is called the *Yoga Sutras*, in which this godhead concept is called *Ishvara*. Although it is abstract, esoteric in nature, and very difficult to explain, in a nutshell Ishvara is a concept of a god that is said to be the ultimate source of creation and perfect state of being.[3] Yoga, and other religions that believe in this godhead concept (which is called different names depending upon the tradition), say we all came from this god and we are all on a spiritual path to ultimately lose our sense of self and reunite (or *yoke*) with it completely. The practice of yoga is one way of doing so.

This includes the yoga most of us know—the one involving cute pants and a squishy mat. It is one of the practices on this yogic path. It is a type of movement meditation, meaning that the goal of the practice is to bring the body and mind into a state of relaxed openness that allows practitioners to yoke with the spiritual realm.

Movement is important; so is sound. The *Yoga Sutras* tells us that *Om* is the sound representation of Ishvara.[4] Chanting "Om" is an invitation, or invocation of this god.[5] In my yoga teacher training, I was instructed that every class we ever taught should start with chanting "Om" three times. It was important for teachers to introduce additional mantras (or chants) representing and invoking other energies and deities, especially as the students became more open to the practice, which was initially awkward-feeling.

From the training I learned that the traditional mantras have special power to invoke heightened meditative states, so teaching them was essential. The teacher could share the meaning of a chant, or just teach the foreign words and/or tones *without* explaining the meaning. Students did not need to know the meaning of a chant to experience its profound spiritual effects; they simply needed to chant it.

The same thing was taught during my time at the Buddhist center, but in regard to Tibetan Buddhist mantras. I noticed many similarities between the two, and recognized them as equal paths to truth. Through the new yoga prayers or mantras, I deepened my practice immensely, and was thrilled to have yet another tool by which to share peace and love with others.

By the time I returned from India, I was a certified yoga teacher and master level reiki energy healer. My meditative practice had never been so deep. But even beyond the meditative waves of peaceful energy and supernatural experiences, nothing validated my place on the right path of truth and understanding more than the everyday feelings of balance, peace, and love that seemed to correlate with regular practice and meditation.

It seemed to me that feeling, experiencing, and sharing love and peace was the point of this life.

5
MEETING TYLER

It was a girls' weekend road trip on the Northern California coast—one last hurrah before heading to Montana for the summer. I had just biked ten sweaty miles on the shoulder of a busy highway to retrieve my car from the site of the hoedown we'd wisely left it at the previous night, and we were packing up the car. I hadn't even brushed my teeth yet. I could feel the shots from the night before seeping from my pores. If I had to choose one word to describe myself, *haggard* would not have been strong enough.

There Tyler was in the hotel parking lot, in his white truck with his tousled dark hair and intense eyes, and my ridiculous friends in their silly thrift-store hats striking up conversation. He was gorgeous. I could hear him talking. There was a twinge of something like a sweet drawl to his voice. It was a bit of "southern boy meets California surfer."

I tried to hide behind the open trunk of the car, but I was soon called over and introduced. I could barely make eye contact without blushing. I was sure my teeth were fuzzy. My hair was a ponytail of blonde frizz matted down from the sweaty bike helmet. For all I knew, my makeup from the night before was smeared into abstract art around my eyes.

I was not cute. But much to my amazement, there must have been something about the mess of me that Tyler found appealing.

Unfortunately, that state of mess would become the lingering theme of our relationship. The explosive and immediate chemistry between us quickly devolved into an extremely volatile relationship that seemed destined to fail from day one.

First of all, I was on my way back to Oregon to pack and

head to Montana for the summer. He lived in the town of the said parking lot. But the chemistry between us was like a drug. We traveled back and forth over the summer, trying to make the long-distance thing work right from the beginning. Issues and baggage from our respective past relationships and childhoods made this start very difficult, to say the least.

My own insecurities and, honestly, the poor state of my morals overall, led me to make some pretty horrible decisions before our relationship even became one, technically speaking. My issues reacted with issues from Tyler's past in blistering ways; we never could get past them. The same concerns repeated themselves in long, repeated discussions and arguments about every day and a half. But we loved each other and had such a strong connection so we tried and tried to make it work.

But nothing accomplished what we hoped for. No amount of discussion could dig out the roots of our multi-layered issues. When things were good, they were amazing; and when they were bad, they were excruciating.

Before I get into the next part of the story with Tyler and me, it's important to understand something about my general outlook toward life. Anyone close to me knows that I am typically the farthest from depression that you could imagine being. I'm happy and I love my life. I've tried to always remember how very lucky and blessed I have been, and I've made it a point to be thankful for everything I have.

I had it pretty easy, and I greatly appreciated it. Other than the normal, teary teenage outbursts of youth, there was only one other brief time in my "life before Tyler" when I began feeling depressed. It happened in my mid-twenties and was the obvious result of over-partying and over-drinking. Apparently, when you pump a depressant into your body almost every day for eight months, it makes you feel . . . depressed. (Weird, I know.) Other than that, I was almost always happy. And it wasn't the "I have to pretend to be happy," kind of happy. I was really, truly, genuinely happy.

There *was* something kind of strange, though, that I'd never told anyone until after the stuff happened that I'm about to share: every once in a while during the prior few years before I met Tyler, I would have strange, totally spontaneous, and surprising random thoughts of the sweet relief that dying might bring.

Because I had been so happy and had experienced nothing close to feelings of depression, those random thoughts shocked me. For example, I'd be crossing the street, see a car coming, and wonder what it would be like if the car hit me. The thought would bring a strange sense of relief. It's hard to explain, but a part of me would ponder how good it would feel to be done with all of this.

Whenever this happened, I felt the same surprise because I didn't feel like there was anything in particular I wanted to be done with. Nor was I feeling depressed or even bummed out. It was an odd sense of, "Man, I'm just so . . . . done . . . with this planet." My mind would flash questions like, "Wouldn't it just be so nice to be free from this body? What is the *point* of all of this?"

These thoughts would fly in randomly, and at the strangest times: While having a glass of wine with friends, it would happen: "Man, what's the point? It would be great to sink into nothingness and leave this body behind."

To be perfectly clear, I never actually considered letting a car hit me or anything like that. It was just the initial split-second when the thought flashed in my mind. I never told anyone about it. In retrospect, I noticed that when I returned from India, these instances grew in frequency and strength.

Okay, back to Tyler and me. The discussions that turned into arguments and verbal attacks eventually occurred so frequently that I became depressed. I am not trying to paint Tyler as the bad guy here. I understood his issues and his reasons not to trust. But I also acknowledged that the issues we were facing were deeper and about more than any actions I took in our relationship. We were dealing with bigger things; and they needed to change.

But nothing was changing. I became more and more frustrated each time Tyler distrusted me or brought up what I had done. I was so tired of it that I began to feel generally and increasingly exhausted. Sometimes in the midst of our multiple-hours-long conversations about whatever the issue was, I would start thinking about how much I wanted to sink into the earth and be finished—anything that would stop me from feeling the way his verbal attacks made me feel.

Things were getting really bad. So why didn't I break up with Tyler if I was so miserable? Indeed, that would have seemed the logical thing to do. But as bad as the bad times were, the good times seemed to balance them out. I just wanted the good times to last forever. And I felt responsible for the bad times since they seemed to stem from my poor choices before and during the beginning of our relationship.

Meanwhile, Tyler said that if he just had time to work through the issues, the bad times would eventually go away, and we'd be left with nothing but happy days. Because I felt so responsible and wanted so much for us to have the healthy relationship I believed possible, I thought the least I could do was stick it out through the bad times and let Tyler work through his issues.

But it was draining me.

At one point, I was absolutely desperate for Tyler to stop speaking cruel and painful words. The meanness was so excruciating that I wanted to do everything in my power to make it stop. As desperate as it was, my pleading didn't work. Frustration boiled in my veins and burst forth in a rush of energy that ended with my grabbing whatever was in reach and throwing it at him. I don't even remember what I threw or whether it hit him; I just remember being extremely troubled by the fact that I had reached a point where I was reacting this way.

My throwing whatever I threw did not faze Tyler. The verbal attack continued with a remark so cutting that I reached out and hit him in the face. My behavior caught me off guard. I never saw myself as being capable of hitting someone like that. I hated violence and loved everything. I saved bugs!

But hot rage boiled in my blood. Tyler had told me that he'd seen hatred in me for some time, but I thought he was just being a jerk. After all, I was full of peace and love. Yet I was starting to see what he meant. I glimpsed the hatred I never thought I had.

Where had it come from? When did it begin? There were times in my life when I had yelled and said hurtful things in arguments. But except for a one-time roll-around with my sister during our teens (in an argument over clothes, of course), I had never been in a disagreement that turned physical. Yet at this point the combination of rage and the overwhelming urge to make it stop grew exponentially.

This is when the first "thing" happened.

6
RUNNING ON THE EDGE

Tyler and I had been arguing all day, and all day the day before. I was exhausted from it. Nothing I said or did stopped his clawing words. I had been telling him for weeks that when he did this, it made me want to sink down and disappear into the ground. I was that serious and that sick of it.

Tyler's stone-faced expression convinced me that he didn't believe how serious I was; or if he did, he was too engulfed in his own pain to care. Strangely enough, leaving the relationship wasn't a real option for me. I still felt like the whole thing was my fault, and we could get through it if I just persevered long enough. Because I believed my actions caused him to feel the way he did, I felt I owed him that much—even though I knew my perseverance was dragging me lower than I'd ever been.

ৎ ৎ ৎ

We decided that driving out to the beach and taking a walk would create a break in the arguing. But as we approached the pull-off to park, Tyler opened his mouth and spewed a stream of words so fierce and sudden that they hit me like a hard slap across the face. My heart reacted instantly, shooting lightning-hot adrenaline through my veins. I hated Tyler for being capable of hurting me this way, especially when he knew full well the limits to which I had already been pushed; and I hated myself for having made the horrid decisions that ruined what might have been an amazing foundation in our relationship.

Exhausted and done with all of it, a thought popped into my mind: "Go jump in the ocean."

This thought had come up before in prior weeks. Exasperated, I had told Tyler in the middle of some recent arguments that his words made me want to jump into the ocean and never come out. I also remembered my near-drowning experience in Costa Rica some years earlier, and how peaceful it had seemed.

"I'm so done with this," I murmured under my breath, eyes fixed on my hands fumbling in my lap while my thumbnail softly rubbed into the pad of my pointer finger. My adrenaline-fueled anger boiled up faster than I had time to recognize. With suddenness it bubbled over and out of me.

I turned to Tyler, angry and short. "I'm jumping in the ocean."

My words flowed calmly, quickly, decidedly. I pulled the handle of the door and darted toward the hills of beach grass separating the truck from the shore. I sprinted at full speed, energized by rage and a total lack of care. All I wanted was an end to the pain.

As my legs carried me, everything slowed down and my thoughts split into two distinct categories: On one side, it felt good to run through the grass, and I longed to jump into the cold surf. Mostly, I wanted Tyler to know how serious I was so he would stop. I wasn't thinking I would drown. What I really wanted was for him to jump in after me, bring me back to shore, and take my pleading to heart. I thought that if he believed I was serious about this and realized how far he had pushed me, he would stop. Perhaps then he would finally trust, once and for all, that I was truly sorry. (It is, by the way, very embarrassing for me to admit all of this. I am completely aware of how ridiculously unhealthy and irrational my train of thought was. But it's the truth of the matter; so it needs to be told.) A small part of me didn't even care whether I got sucked into the ocean and died. I longed to be done with the whole mess. I simply did...not...care.

My second train of thought showed me just how low I had sunk. As I raced through the beach grass toward the ocean, my rational thoughts interjected: "What on Earth are you thinking? Jessica! This is absolutely crazy! This is not you. You love life. Why are you doing this? You need to stop. You need to stop now."...

As I raced through the beach grass toward the ocean, my rational thoughts interjected: "*What* on Earth are you thinking? Jessica! This is absolutely crazy! This is not you. You love life. Why are you doing this? You need to stop. You need to stop *now*."

During the whole slow-motion sprint through the beach grass, my thoughts battled back and forth; but the jumping-in-the-ocean ones seemed to be winning. I wanted to do it. I pumped myself up, trying to push away the more rational train of thought and tuning into the thoughts I knew would push me. "Just do it. Do it! It will feel so good to just jump in." The idea was almost pleading.

The two trains of thought were so strong and so fervently opposite. I noted the strange dichotomy as I ran closer to the ocean. Cresting the hill that opened onto the sandy beach, I picked up my pace. "Just do it. Just do it," my thoughts chanted. I pushed out all other thoughts as I charged toward the water. I was going to do it, and it felt so good, so freeing.

Just as I neared the sea, a different thought broke through my wall. It was simple, but carried overwhelming authority.

"Stop!"

At that moment, I noticed something that just happened to be on the edge of the surf: a massive, old-growth driftwood stump that had rooted itself deeply into the sand where the tide met the shore. Instead of lunging into the water, I collapsed onto the stump, my knees sinking into the sand, my body overcome by sobs.

What was I thinking? How had I let myself get to this point? Who was this person I was becoming? I sobbed in total emotional exhaustion as the next set of waves pounded the shoreline and soaked me from the waist down. I didn't have the energy to care or move, even though the seawater surged and swirled around my legs.

I heard Tyler yelling as he charged over the hill and onto the beach: "Jessica! Get out of the water! Jessica, the waves are coming up; get out of the water!"

But I really didn't care to listen. Sobs shook my shoulders and my legs felt rubbery beneath me when Tyler pulled me back to dry sand. "Come on. Let's go. You're soaked." He was not impressed.

I gulped air and tears flowed down my cheeks as I made my way back to the car by myself, Tyler a hurried distance ahead.

Never had I felt so atrociously and completely alone.

7
WAKE-UP CALL

Things were fairly quiet back at home as we settled into the awkwardness of what had happened. I was still exhausted and more than a little shocked with my actions as I tried to process the thoughts I'd had earlier when I ran for the beach. How had I let myself reach such a point? How had these irrational thoughts taken hold?

Although I regretted my wild dash for the ocean, I still hoped that Tyler had at last realized how serious I was about ending the unhealthy patterns in our relationship. But as night fell, I listened in disbelief as he started on the same thing all over again. He wanted to keep reliving the same story. He didn't recognize how far over the line we had gone. We had been there before, and had already spent many days' worth of time rehashing it. Yet he wanted to relive the horrid details *again*. The worst part was that Tyler still didn't believe me. There seemed to be no possible way to convince him of what I was feeling or of how sorry I was for my past mistakes.

All hope drained from my being so that I could not even care enough to be upset. This is what it was like to have reached my limit and gone past it. I had been sitting atop the bed in Tyler's studio, but sank down until I was lying on the bed, consumed by something I had never quite experienced: an intense, total and utter lack of care. Then, as I wished I could sink through the mattress and into the ground, something bizarre happened. Because of the nature of what transpired, it is very hard to explain. But I'll do the best I can within the limits of our language.

ও   ও   ও

I was lying on my back when, out of nowhere, my stomach contracted so intensely that it lifted my upper torso and then dropped me back to the bed. I don't want to use the term *mini-convulsion*, but in a way, it is the only one I can think of that comes close to describing what I experienced. It was not a voluntary action; nor had I ever seen or heard of anything like it. Neither was I thinking of Tyler at that moment or trying to convince him of how serious I was. Unlike the earlier incident, this was not an attempt to get his attention. The truth is that I was no longer concerned whether he believed me or not. In fact, I did not care about *anything at all.*

Just as it is difficult to explain my experiences in working with spiritual energy, it is also incredibly hard to describe this event. The best I can do is to say that it felt like some kind of energy was sending waves of physical and emotional numbness through my body. The contractions were somehow involved in this energy. It felt consuming and good.

I was completely aware that my body was doing strange, convulsive things, but I did not care enough to try to determine the cause. It was as though I had dropped into a peaceful, meditative state in which I remained aware of my surroundings and everything that was happening to me, while feeling deeply removed from it all.

Tyler knelt next to me and spoke urgently. "Should I call an ambulance?" he asked in horror.

"Should he?" I wondered inwardly. I didn't know, nor did I care. My eyes were fixed straight ahead, and I could not make myself care enough to move them. Could I? The question interested me, but it didn't bother me in the slightest to think that I might be unable to move my eyes. It just didn't matter. I had a vague flash of a thought that I might be dying. It felt kind of nice; the meditative sense of detachment made me feel peaceful.

I noticed an overwhelming sense that something was there, and became aware of a presence in the upper right-hand corner of the room. It didn't freak me out because I was used to working with energies and spirits. It exuded feelings of peace and love, as of a guide. It wanted me to accompany it, and I liked the idea. At the same time, a strange undertone kept me vaguely aware that I might be dying as I sank deeper and deeper into the numbness. But nothing about that bothered me. There was a peaceful presence of light and love. Everything was okay.

Although I was totally aware of what was going on, I was also completely removed from feeling any emotions that should have normally accompanied such an experience. Once again, words are inadequate. But the strange dichotomy thing resurfaced: My primary desire was to sink into the numbness and let it consume me. I was drawn to it as though it were a magnet. But as much as I wanted to surrender to its powerful pull, something else drew me away from it and kept bringing my attention back to Tyler's terrified, frantic pleas to God to keep me from dying. The thought popped into my mind that people loved me and would be hurt if I surrendered. I acknowledged the reality of love in my mind and in my thoughts, but I *felt* no love. As weird as it was and as hard as it is to explain, I felt nothing—only a blissful, numbing nothingness.

It was interesting to me that Tyler somehow knew I might be dying. Despite the fact that I was numb and "mini-convulsing," I was wide-awake and fully aware (at least I thought I was). Yet I didn't care about the possibility of dying. I had dropped into a state of meditation in which I was simply observing but not feeling. There was no attachment, only the splitting of my thoughts in two directions.

My eyes remained fixed on the ceiling, but my attention went to Tyler, who was still pleading and desperate beside me. "You love him," a thought told me. Intellectually speaking, I knew that I loved him and I did not want him to feel any pain. But I could not *feel* love. I was numb to any love for anyone I had ever known. I was numb to any love for myself, and to any feeling of any sort. I was totally detached, blissfully and completely devoid of feeling.

My thoughts continued to battle. One side was pleading, soft, parental, loving, gentle, and kind: "Jessica, you don't feel love, but you know love. You *know* you love Tyler. You know he loves you. Don't do this."

I knew this side of my thinking was right even though the other side—the magnet that pulled me toward numbness—felt better. Tyler was right in front of me. His face inches from mine, he pleaded with me to move my eyes and look at him. I wondered whether I could. Feeling nothing, and wanting to stay that way, I was also aware that the thought of reason—the loving, sweet thought that was trying to draw me out of this deadened state—was relentless. "Just move your eyes, Jessica," it said.

Patient and soft, it persisted. Annoyed by knowing it was right, and frustrated that I could not be left alone in the consuming numbness, I relented by focusing all my energy on my eyes until they moved to look at Tyler. I thought it was weird to have to concentrate so hard just to make my eyes obey. Tyler reacted like someone watching the first breath of a person who was being resuscitated. "Oh, thank God!" His cry reflected frantic hope.

"Good, Jessica! Good!" Then he switched his focus to my limp right hand in his. "Now squeeze my finger! Squeeze my finger! Can you squeeze my finger, Jessica?"

"Of course I can squeeze your finger," I thought. So I focused on my hand and squeezed hard. But nothing happened. Though I squeezed with all my strength, my fingers moved so feebly that anyone not holding my hand would have wondered whether they had moved at all. This startled and captured my attention.

"What the heck?" I thought. "Why can't I move my hands when I want to?" Up to that point, I had not realized the extent of the *physical* numbness. I thought that if I really wanted to pull myself out of it, I would be able to move. But I discovered that I could barely move at all. This so shocked me that even though I was still emotionally numb, I focused my total attention on clenching my fingers around Tyler's. I squeezed and squeezed, growing a little stronger each time, until Tyler was satisfied that my grip had returned to normal.

Then he moved to my other hand and asked me to squeeze it. In the same way, the feeling returned to my other hand. Once both my eyes and hands could move, he directed my attention to my toes. In this same manner, Tyler walked me through the waking up of my entire body.

I did not want to return from the numbness, but having my parts revived was like waking up from a dream. My attention seemed to be pulled out of the meditative state of consuming numbness and toward the unusual thing that had happened to my body.

Once I was able to move my limbs, life seemed to flood into me again, both physically and mentally. Part of me was disappointed to see the tide of peaceful numbness recede; but I was also overwhelmed and confused by the power of what had just happened. Within minutes, I regained full control over my body. I had channeled energies in my healing practices and worked with spirits for years, but this was the only time anything like *this* had ever happened to me. It very much felt like death had danced with me, and then allowed me to return to my life.

I didn't know what to make of the incident. Neither did Tyler. We were both overwhelmed, slightly terrified, and grateful that nothing worse had happened. We didn't talk about the experience much because we were so creeped out by it. So we tried to forget it, chalking it up to a divine intervention of some kind—a wake-up call to do something about our problems.

We had no idea that it would pale in comparison to the event that was just ahead.

8
THE RANCH

Tyler and I knew we needed to get to the root of our issues and dig them out if we wanted to survive together. Within a couple weeks of the incident at the beach, we both had breaks in our work schedules. The timing lined up perfectly for us to visit Don and Dawn, some friends of my parents who do counseling at their ranch up the Smith River in southern Oregon. Their counseling program had such great results when they lived in Alaska that local judges began to require it as a rehabilitation option to some convicted criminals. The program went to the root of the person's early years and explained how human development can be stunted by things that occur during childhood.

Neither Tyler nor I had suffered severe abuse as children, but we definitely had stuff to deal with and work on. The idea was that once the root of an issue was understood and addressed, we could learn how to break unhealthy patterns and replace them with new approaches.

That sounded great to me, except for one thing: Don and Dawn were Christians. No way would I agree to get Bible-thumped in a counseling session! But my mom assured me that they would respect my views and not press me about religion. She reminded me that, as counselors, they were totally capable of helping people without pushing their beliefs on them.

With some hesitation, I decided to give them a chance. After all, the timing lined up so perfectly with the breaks in our schedules, especially right before our big move-in together. It seemed foolish not to get some counseling. "But if they push Jesus on me *once*," I warned my mom, "I am out of there."

Obviously we couldn't go through Don and Dawn's whole multi-month program in a few days' time. Nor were we willing to commit to any extended period of counseling. So the plan

47

was that Tyler would work with Don and Dawn on the first day. I would arrive the following day to work with Dawn while Don and Tyler did something else. On the third day, we would come together as a group.

When I arrived, Tyler had been there a full day without me, and I felt that he was being a little odd and standoffish toward me. Dawn took me aside and assured me that Tyler had just been through a lot in his session. She explained that it was natural for him to need a little space right now. That made sense to me.

We split into our two groups: Tyler and Don worked outside while Dawn and I discussed the process of development. As morning slipped into afternoon, a lot of light was shed on why I acted and responded in certain ways, and how my childhood influenced the person I had become. I was feeling good about what was being accomplished, and as my mom promised, no one pressured me to become a Christian.

After lunch Tyler and I had our first opportunity to be alone while Don and Dawn attended to things on the ranch. I thought Tyler was still acting *very* strangely. He was talking cautiously and fumbling awkwardly with his hands in the pockets of his jeans. Finally, he lifted his eyes to meet mine.

"Look," he began. "I want you to know that I had a really powerful experience here. And . . ." his gaze returned to the grass. "I am not saying this to sound threatening or anything, but I just want you to know. If you don't have a similar experience, I . . . I love you, but I just don't know whether things will work out for us."

What? I was confused by Tyler's statement. This was the same guy who said the day before that he wanted to spend the rest of his life with me. Now, unless I had a similar experience to his "powerful experience," he might be unable to be with me? His words seemed harsh. After all, I was trying to get as much out of this as I could, but I could only get out of it what I could get out of it. Why was he being so weird?

I took a deep breath. "Tyler, I'm really trying not to get

defensive right now. I mean, I'm putting in as much effort as I can and I'll get out of it what I can. But I don't see how you can tell me that if I don't have the same experience as you, then you're not sure it's going to work out."

I just didn't get it. I was open to learning and changing. And Tyler had been the one to bring up the whole marriage thing, not me. How could he go from that point to this in such a short time?

"Don't get defensive," he returned. "It's just that I'm seeing things differently, and I have to do what I know in my heart is right for me." He was talking in his usual ambiguous way, but being even more vague than usual. I sighed in confusion, but didn't push the issue, trusting that whatever it was would come out in time.

We were grateful for the break in conversation when Don approached and motioned toward the four-wheeler. "Tyler, why don't you two take a ride down to that waterfall we went to yesterday and show Jessica?"

We both climbed on and Tyler started the engine, making conversation impossible as the brisk air whirled a chill against my face. When Tyler parked, I could tell he had been thinking the whole time about what he was going to say. He was being so weird, so tentative with his words, like he was afraid to say too much or the wrong thing or leak a secret.

Then it hit me. I knew why he was being so weird. I couldn't believe I hadn't figured it out sooner. It was so obvious! The odd talk about me not getting the same thing out of it, and the whole bit about following his heart—they must have turned him into a Christian!

It made perfect sense. I knew Tyler had grown up Catholic, so he had some foundation in what Jesus was about. He'd even mentioned going back to church a few times before we got together. That stopped, of course, once we officially started seeing each other. Oh, was I livid! I knew that Don and Dawn had done Christian missionary work, and that they were really,

really Christian. I definitely would never have agreed to this counseling if I thought for a moment that they would turn my boyfriend into a Christian.

Could it get any worse? There he was, talking about following what he knew in his heart he had to do for himself, when just yesterday *I* was the only thing he wanted in his heart. A day ago, he talked about spending the rest of his life with me. Today something else took precedence over me. The only logical explanation was that they had turned him into *one of them*.

The realization left me fuming. I sent my boyfriend up here for one day for counseling, and they turned him into the one type of person I could not stand: a judgmental, fake, hypocritical Christian! I took a deep, slow breath, inwardly, so Tyler wouldn't know I'd figured out his secret. I didn't know how to bring it up anyway.

I imagined him in a white shirt and skinny tie, yelling "Hallelujah!" and pretentiously slapping the back of some plastic-looking guy in a collared shirt, while they both "fake laughed" at a stupid joke about gay people or Mormons. Maybe Tyler even told the joke. Ugh!

Why had I left him up here alone? All the judging, all the hypocrisy, everything I detested about religion—and here he was, buying into the *one* religion that I thought enveloped all those qualities!

I was blood-boiling furious!

My inner anger surged only momentarily before I calmed down, comforting myself with the fact that I really didn't know anything for sure. But I *knew*. It's like being at a funeral and holding onto that speck of hope in the back of your mind that the person you're commemorating will come running down the aisle and you'll realize the whole thing was a horrible, tasteless joke. Deep down you know it's not going to happen.

I consoled myself with the possibility that the situation

50   THE SHATTERING

wasn't as bad as I suspected. Maybe Tyler would be satisfied simply praying to Jesus without having to constantly judge me and my actions and everyone else in the world. Maybe he would never yell, "Amen, brother!"

I could deal with that.

The truth was that I had wanted to let go of my resentments toward Jesus—not toward Christians, but toward Jesus. I had recently grown to accept him as a beautiful and amazing spirit, a teacher of peace and love, and an incredibly powerful healer. I remembered the Jesus I had read about in the Bible as a kid, and the countless nights I'd spent getting down on my little knees or crawling into my bed and talking to him as a father and friend. I had recently been giving a lot of thought to how it wasn't his fault that people corrupted his message of peace and love. I knew it wasn't fair for me to associate him with the hypocritical, judgmental people who claimed to be his followers. I thought how saddened Jesus must be by the way they tarnished his life's work by being such fakes.

Maybe Tyler wasn't going super-Christian on me; maybe he just wanted to start praying to Jesus. Yup, it was best to just simmer down and wait to see how the next day would pan out.

Later that night at dinner, Don and Dawn shared stories of their ministries in Alaska. They talked about how great Jesus was and how he brought healing and peace to so many people there. Surprisingly, I wasn't repulsed by the conversation. It was nice to hear from two people who were working with Jesus, just as I had worked with my guides and other spirits to do good things in the world.

As we sat around the table, something strange began to happen. I felt a longing in my heart, an overwhelming kind of sadness. It was that dull, pulsing ache that accompanies intensely missing someone you love. Sitting there, I realized the source. It was a longing for those times I had spent with Jesus during my childhood and in my teens. I missed the comfort I had found in them. I had loved reading the Bible and praying to him. He had been very real to me; I talked to him all the time and truly loved him. In those days, I simply believed because I didn't know any reason not to. It was before I learned to question, and prior to becoming dependent on the seeming spiritual validation I got from feelings, energies, or experiences.

Jesus had been with me through all those hard times growing up; back when I simply trusted him. I felt a twinge in my heart—an ache of wanting that relationship back.

For a year or so, I had been giving some thought to picking one path within my spiritual practices and sticking with it. It wasn't that I had ping-ponged from one tradition to the next. Since turning away from Christianity, everything I studied fell under the same umbrella of spiritual thought. Each of the Eastern traditions and other meditative, energetic, and spiritual paths I had studied all seemed to have a lot in common. From my perspective, the spiritual walk was like climbing up a mountain. There were many paths to the top—many ways to reach God and a state of enlightenment or oneness with him (or the "divine," or "Ishvara", or "the Universe" or "Brahman" or whatever you wanted to call it). I considered the Buddha to have taught just one of them, the yogis another, and various spiritual leaders imparted countless others.

I had only recently accepted the idea that Jesus also taught one of those paths. For a long time, I had discounted his teachings completely because of the lack of any physical feelings and esoteric spiritual experiences during the many years I had prayed only to him. There was no comparison with the intense experiences and surges of peaceful energy accompanying my meditations and work with other spirits or energies. After praying to Jesus for years, even though I had seen answers to prayers, I had not a single supernatural experience or any physical validation that I was "connecting" with anything or anyone. With Jesus, I had to rely totally on faith.

Because Jesus hadn't given me the types of results I had

from working with other spirits, I came to believe that he was either not real or not powerful. Yet during the previous couple of years, that outlook had been changing, and two fractures opened in my hardness toward him.

9
THE FRACTURES BEGIN

The first crack in my hardened shell against Jesus occurred during an adventure through the Balkans with some friends a year or so prior. We were exploring a small coastal town in Slovenia, a lovely country a little larger than Connecticut that borders Northeastern Italy. The whole town seemed to be built on the side of a hill, perched high above the sea. Tourist season had just ended, and we meandered up the deserted cobblestone maze of skinny roads and path. When we reached the top, our view opened into a spectacular spread: the picturesque town beneath us to one side, and the bright Adriatic Sea on the other.

In front of us was a grassy clearing. Just beyond that, an ancient-looking church appeared to be in ruins, its paint chipping and its doors decidedly locked. I assumed it had been closed long ago, so I focused on the breathtaking view. It felt like we were standing in some unknown moment in history, alone atop this panorama. My thoughts took me to the men who must have kept watch from this point for threats coming in from the sea. I reflected on the generations of people over hundreds of years who traveled up this hill to pray to their God inside those walls. The weddings, the sorrows, the wars—this little spot demanded a respect for its history alone.

We finally snapped some photos and pulled ourselves away from the stunning view. As we made our way down the cobblestone walkway alongside the church, we noticed the only person we had seen in quite a while: a little old woman hobbling toward us from the opposite end of the path. Her feet shuffled under her round body, causing the large basket draped beneath her arm to sway from side to side. The scene was like a postcard—the quaint village grandmother teetering up the hillside's aged rock path. Even from a distance, we could tell that her weathered face was crinkled with years of stories. Just as we were about to pass by, the woman paused at the locked side door of the church, lifted her kind eyes, and motioned with grandmotherly authority for us to follow. She was unlocking the old church!

My three friends and I exchanged raised-brow glances, amazed at our luck as her wrinkled fingers rummaged through a set of keys, finally sliding one into the ancient-looking lock. Expecting to enter a rundown, spider-webbed interior, we eagerly followed behind the woman and entered a dark, tiny room. "It must be the utility room," I thought, as my eyes adjusted to the darkness.

The woman motioned for us to stop while she hurried to flip switches here and there. Moments later, her soft eyes twinkled as she opened another door and turned to face us. She smiled warmly and nodded her head toward the opening, uttering something I assumed could be roughly translated as "Enter."

I smiled my gratitude and lowered my head in thanks, then rounded the corner of the interior to find myself astonished—we had walked into the scene of an enchanted storybook. A soft symphony danced from hidden speakers and echoed throughout an ornate, glowingly lit cathedral. Exquisite paintings decorated the walls. My eyes soaked in the finely-detailed beauty that surrounded the empty wooden pews.

We each wandered in our own directions in awe and reverent silence. I found myself drawn to the front of the church toward a giant crucifix. I stood there staring up at the cross with the body representing Jesus hanging on it, the apex of everything in the room. I didn't want to leave. It was incredible, and so peaceful. Finally, I realized that I had probably been there for an awkwardly long time, hogging the best part of the place. So I pulled myself away to an empty pew where I sat in stillness. The experience was amazing—and it was in a Christian church.

The thought fractured something in me. It was the first crack in my shell that had hardened against Jesus. In that pew I realized that I had been associating him with his followers and resenting *him* for the way some people had corrupted his teachings and acted like hypocrites in his name. The unfairness of my attitude struck me.

Around the time of this incident, I was working with what I believed to be my guides and angels in my spiritual practice. I would be moving into a Buddhist center in a few months, so I certainly wasn't ready to start working with Jesus. But this was the first time since my discovery of the Metaphysics/New Age section of the bookstore that I realized and acknowledged the idea of Jesus being a powerful spirit that I could work with. For me, it was a pretty big step.

Next I was introduced to a book that widened the fissure. It was a story written by a Christian author about a vaguely supernatural experience with Jesus. I was never sure whether the author was describing a dream or reality. Either way, it was right up my alley, as spiritual experiences go. Regardless of what really happened, the author was writing about an esoteric experience with Jesus. I was amazed that a Christian would be open to exploring such a thing, and that Jesus would be capable of it.

Since those first fractures in my shell, I hadn't given any serious thought to the subject of Jesus, but I *had* been considering selecting one path to expedite my spiritual journey to the "mountaintop." My natural tendency to try everything before I made a decision about anything was getting ridiculous. I would travel up one route; then try another, and another, and another.

With so many similarities shared by these paths, and because they all operated under one umbrella, I was progressing in my spiritual quest. I figured I would eventually make my way to the top of the mountain by bushwhacking my own way to the top—a little on this path, a little on that. But I had started to wonder whether forging my own way from trail to trail made sense. So many trails had already been blazed and groomed. If I wanted to expedite my spiritual growth and reach the summit, why not just pick one?

The Fractures Begin

10
BACK AT THE RANCH

Back at the dinner table with Don and Dawn, I stared down at my hands folded in my lap. Conversation became a blur in the background as a thought came to mind that I'd never had before. The simplicity of the rationale clicked in an instant. I was actually slightly surprised I hadn't thought of it before. I had been working with several great guides and spirits, but my relationship with all of them was relatively new. I would bring new ones in and let others go, working with one guide for a while, then an angel, then a Buddhist or Hindu deity, etc. But I hadn't worked with any one entity consistently for any number of years. So how deep was my connection with them, really?

It made sense to stop wasting my time with these "acquaintance" spirits, and work solely with Jesus. He was the one spirit I *knew*, the one who knew me the best because I had prayed to him during the foundational years of my life. From the time I was old enough to form thoughts, all the way into early adulthood, Jesus was the one I talked to. Even when my prayers became fewer and fewer, he was the one to whom they were directed. He remained the only one until I exchanged my Bible for the Metaphysics/New Age section of the bookstore.

Now after all these years, my heart ached to reestablish the relationship, and my mind continued in its reasoning. When I actually considered his life's work, Jesus seemed to be the highest spirit of all. I loved that he was so dedicated to helping and healing others. I thought about all the miraculous healings Jesus performed time and again, as the Bible accounts record. I also thought about the love he preached and the way he died on the cross (even though I no longer understood why). Jesus even predicted his own death and resurrection, and then rose back to life after dying in the exact manner he had foretold. Neither Buddha nor any other guides, angels, or spirits ever did anything like that. The fact that there are multiple documents recording that Jesus was a real, living, breathing person only a couple thousand years ago and that all that *actually* happened is absolutely incredible.

It was starting to seem pointless to even bother working with these other energies when Jesus was the ultimate master of love and healing energy—the exact things I wanted to cultivate and share with others. I remembered that the Bible says, "God is love,"[6] and that Jesus claimed to be God's Son, an extension of God himself. That meant that he claimed to be the absolute, purest form of love.

Of course, I wasn't sure what I believed about the whole God thing. Maybe it was just a symbol for uniting with the "divine," or "the Universe," or whatever you wanted to call it. But I decided there at the table that it didn't matter; I was going to follow Jesus' path. If he would have me back, the most sensible thing to do was to pick his path—as long as I didn't have to go to church or listen to Christian music or anything like that. I would study the Bible myself, but without becoming a typical, crazy, plastic-looking Christian.

All of these thoughts flowed while Don and Dawn told their stories over dinner. I was half listening and half thinking about Jesus and the ache in my heart for him when Dawn paused her story. Perhaps it was my lack of participation in the conversation; or maybe my facial expression gave me away. She was at the point in her story when she had told someone, "Jesus loves you."

She stopped and looked right at me. "Jessica, Jesus loves you, too, you know."

Like a little baby, tears immediately streamed from my eyes. I hurried to wipe them away; I wasn't ready to share what was going on in my heart. My relationship with Jesus (or lack thereof) was personal to me. It felt awkward to talk about it. But I answered Dawn. "I know," I said quietly.

Then, before I could stop them, new words tumbled out with a fresh cascade of tears. "We used to be really close." I tried not to sniffle and pretended that my eyes were fine after a couple of quick dabs with my napkin.

Don and Dawn didn't push any further.

That night, alone in my room, I prayed to Jesus for the first time in so many years that I couldn't even remember how long it had been. I was surprised again at the dull longing in my heart and the tears that spilled down my cheeks. For the first time, I felt truly sorry for the way I had regarded Jesus over the years. Not only had I totally rejected him, but I made fun of his teachings, and even swore by using his name, something I'd never dreamt of doing to any of the angels, guides, or spirits I had worked with.

I apologized with my whole heart, then asked Jesus to take me back. Remembering what the Bible said about forgiveness, I knew that he did. He forgave me. His teaching said so; I remembered that.

Next I prayed to my guides, angels, other spirits, and to the Universe (the all-encompassing term I learned to use in place of *God* to include everything I thought to be of light and love). I thanked them for teaching me so much. "But from now on," I concluded, "I only want to work with Jesus."

I had no idea of the power I had just put into motion with that prayer.

After praying, a thought surfaced to grab the Bible that was on my nightstand and turn to the book of Job. I hadn't read the Bible in years. But I vaguely remembered the story of Job. Why I thought of turning there, I had no idea. But curiously, I did.

"Turn two pages," my thoughts said. I was used to following my intuition, so I smiled and turned two pages.

"Middle of the page, on the right."

Back at the Ranch

I looked down and my eyes landed directly on this verse: "Though one wished to dispute with him, he could not answer him one time out of a thousand. His wisdom is profound, his power is vast. Who has resisted him and come out unscathed?"[7]

I smiled and thanked Jesus for leading me to such an appropriate passage. Yet I did not grasp the depth of that last sentence. If I had realized that it did not refer only to the past, but also to a few weeks into my own future, I would not have been smiling, but terrified. In less than a month, that passage would reveal its full meaning in my life.

11
GOING HOME

I should be very clear that my decision to work with Jesus at that particular time was not in any way determined by my assumption that Tyler had turned into a Christian. Rather, it was a result of the inner workings of my own heart, both during and after our dinner with Don and Dawn.

I still did not know the depths of Tyler's experience. As much as I loved him, I was willing to give him up if we no longer met on the same spiritual page. The issue was that important to me. I couldn't be with someone who was a typical Christian. I felt that all the paths I had gone down had taught me valuable information, and I could not be with someone who judged those paths as being negative.

Nor did I want to start telling people that I had "found Jesus." I cringed at the thought of my mom telling her church friends that I'd "come back to our Lord." I knew she would undervalue all the lessons that yoga, meditation, Buddhism, and everything else had taught me; and I knew people would assume that I finally realized how wrong I had been, and how right they were. That idea was light years from what I actually believed.

As soon as Tyler and I were alone for the drive home, I broached the issue. Much to my relief, we seemed close enough to being on the same page that I could see our relationship working out. I breathed a massive sigh of relief.

He didn't, however, buy into my idea that the other spirits I worked with were also paths to truth. "Well, Jess, I mean…who else died for everyone?" Tyler asked.

He had a point. Jesus hadn't just died; he also came back to life. No one else did that. Still, Tyler did seem to acknowledge that I had learned valuable lessons on my path. I could live with that.

We talked about our new views and about how we wanted to live our lives. Everything seemed to line up pretty well. He was the same non-tie-wearing Tyler. He wanted Jesus and the Bible to be more central in his life, but he didn't necessarily want church and religion.

"Phew!" I thought. "Just like me."

Per Don and Dawn's suggestion, we decided that we would start reading the Bible and praying together, but that was all. It was exactly what we both wanted. We didn't have to start saying words like hallelujah or singing old hymns. We laughed in our relief and talked about our experiences the whole way home, giddy at our new understandings. We had new hope that being on the same page spiritually would be the glue that held us together.

Weeks into it, our new plan was working amazingly well. In our final session before returning home, I had told Don and Dawn about my resolution. But I was careful to reinforce the idea that I was "not a regular Christian or anything" and I didn't "believe exactly like other Christians." I tried to be as stern but inoffensive in my tone as possible. "I just want to start reading the Bible and working with Jesus. That's all."

Don and Dawn didn't push anything more than that. They encouraged us to pray and read the Bible aloud together. "Proverbs and Luke are good places to start," they suggested. They smiled warmly and said that reading and praying together would be extremely helpful to our relationship.

They were so right. We prayed together almost every day. We were really good about reading, always squeezing it in sometime during the day. We did manage, however, to whittle our assignment down to just Luke. We were doing the bare minimum: one chapter a day total, alternating who would read aloud. I never really wanted to read aloud, so I pawned it off on Tyler as much as possible. I still found it hard to pray out loud, too. I cringed at the sound of my voice saying the name *Jesus*.

It reminded me of all those people I didn't want to be like. I felt quite badly about it, and prayed that he would help me get rid of my resentments toward him.

Meanwhile, Tyler and I were getting along better than we ever had. Don and Dawn had also talked us into abstaining from physical intimacy for at least a few months so we could focus on developing our relationship. It all seemed to be working. During the month or so after we started reading the Bible together, we experienced only a couple of the old non-trusting incidents, but the intensity was nothing like it had been before. Each time it happened, we prayed together, read the Bible, and talked about it afterwards, which was miraculous for us.

I was in awe, really, to see how much better things were. Tyler had been bringing up marriage for some time, but in light of all our changes, started broaching the subject with more frequency. Our relationship was finally getting to where we had hoped it would go.

As we read and prayed every day, I did not even notice that my hardness toward Jesus was lessening. But it was. It is also important to mention where we were in our Bible reading, because I believe that what was about to happen and what we were reading were probably connected.

The book of Luke goes through Jesus' life from birth to death. I don't know how familiar you are with the Jesus story, but just before he was arrested and horrifically mocked, beaten, and crucified, he and his disciples went to a garden to pray. His disciples were unaware of what was about to happen to him; but because Jesus knew, he experienced natural, human anguish. He knelt and prayed that if there was any other way of accomplishing his assignment, he would be open to having the "cup"—his death sentence—taken from him. In virtually the same breath, he obediently told God, "Not my will, but your will be done."[8]

On the day that I read those words, my heart tugged with

pain at what Jesus must have felt. I imagined the burden he carried over what he knew was coming, and I marveled that he still prayed for His Father's will to be done. His words carried a weight, a "realness" that I'd never experienced. This actually happened, and the story was coming alive to me. To my surprise, tears spilled down my cheeks and my heart pulsed with a dull pain at the overwhelming awfulness Jesus must have felt.

The next day Tyler and I continued reading the story of the crucifixion. I volunteered to read aloud for the second day in a row. I was surprised at how I reacted to the story as I read it. My heart hurt so much with this new "realness" that tears poured down my face and choked me up, forcing me to stop reading numerous times throughout the chapter.

I had prayed that my resentments toward Jesus' name would go away. They began to crumble before my eyes. What I did not know was that within two days, the remainder of the hard shell that had grown around my entire world would completely shatter.

The following day, Tyler finished reading the book of Luke. In its final chapter, Jesus' disciples learn that he has risen from the dead. He preaches to the disciples and is then taken up into heaven. Satan's plan for death is defeated; Jesus beats death and conquers evil.

The very next day, it happened…

12
TREMORS

Most of the arguments between Tyler and me stemmed from his relentless tendency to not believe me about little things. His distrust was due primarily to the decisions I made toward the beginning of our relationship. Now, our new habits of praying and reading the Bible together were helping us. Finally, it looked like we were getting over our "stuff."

But on the afternoon of the day following our reading from Luke about the resurrection, Tyler made a comment—just a little one. Some aspect of my partying past came up and we disagreed over the details. I said in a light way that something happened one way, and Tyler responded along the lines of: "Well, I'm sure it wasn't really like that. I'm sure it was really like this."

In an instant, all the frustration from every past argument we'd ever had surged through my being. I was *furious*. I yelled so loudly the neighbors probably heard me; but I didn't care one bit. Hot, almost palpable rage welled up inside me and spewed out. Once again, my mind split into two distinct thought processes: The rational side said, "Jessica, what are you doing? This isn't you. You don't yell and scream like this. You need to stop." The other side wanted to let it go. The "let it rip" side won out for a while, and I roared my frustration.

Tyler remained completely calm the whole time. He just shook his head in disbelief and said repeatedly that I needed to calm down. His composure eventually shamed me. I knew he was right. I had completely lost my temper. As the fury subsided, I sat on the bed and cried, hugging my knees while rocking slightly back and forth.

The shame of my outburst began to meld with my anger. I noticed what I was doing, and the rocking almost made me laugh. How ridiculous I must have looked! Then I wondered, "Is this what going crazy feels like? I am sobbing and rocking back and forth like a crazy person."

I was deeply angry with myself for losing control, and also surprised at the self-hatred I felt because of it. These were not feelings that I was accustomed to. But as they increased in intensity, I began to loathe myself and dwell on every negative thing about me. The more I thought about it, the more I despised myself. With my thumbnail, I dug into the soft pad of each fingertip, one by one. As the feelings of self-hatred grew stronger, I was surprised at how good it felt to dig my nail into my own flesh. So I started digging a little harder. The pain felt like a release, and I wanted to feel more of it.

"Wow," I thought to myself. "Now you really are going crazy!" I had always heard about people who cut themselves and wondered why they did it. I could not understand people who self-inflicted pain; I thought there was something wrong with them. But there I was, feeling some satisfaction from inflicting pain on myself, and wanting even more of it. It was like something inside me hated me and wanted me to suffer, and the rest of me wanted to go along.

My teeth gnashed in what I can best describe as rage, directed toward myself, as I dug my fingernails deeper and sobbed at the ridiculousness and confusion of the actions and thoughts that were surfacing.

Tyler came to my side on the bed. "Sweetie, what are you doing to yourself?"

I felt embarrassed, like a child caught doing something wrong, when Tyler reached for my hand. But I let him take it. He saw the nail marks pressed firmly into the pads of my fingertips. "Wow, that's messed up," he murmured before he could stop himself. He glanced up quickly and stammered apologetically, "Sorry, I didn't mean that. I just…."

His words didn't even offend me. He was totally right. It was messed up.

"Sweetie," he began again, "Why are you doing this to yourself?"

I could not answer him. The rage had melted away and embarrassment fully replaced it. How had I let myself become so consumed with anger that I would sink to this level? I prided myself on the fact that I loved everything. I valued my calm approach to life, my composure, my peace. That's who I was, or so I thought. I meditated. I was a reiki master. I taught yoga! Where had this upheaval come from? It was horribly embarrassing.

Finally, my embarrassment also settled down, and Tyler and I went about our day in our little home. A bit later, I sheepishly apologized to him for how loudly I'd yelled. After a period of awkwardness and shame, everything seemed fine again.

Before I share what happened next, I need to say this: You might find it hard to accept that it actually happened. I certainly understand why. My own mind searched for every possible psychological and emotional explanation. I really, *really* wanted to believe it was something as mundane and personal as one of these, because then I could sweep the whole experience under the rug, never give it another thought or speak of it to anyone, and get on with my life.

But I can't do that. I know in the depths of my heart, mind, and soul the truth and reality of what took place, and I simply cannot live with myself and not share it. I know it so strongly that it is worth it to me to risk the possibility that some people, perhaps even some of my closest friends, may choose to write it off as a mental and emotional meltdown. I will take that chance. I am willing to shoulder the embarrassment and even the loss of future employment opportunities if a potential employer reads this book and thinks I lost it. It is worth whatever judgments of me will probably be made by some. The risk is worth it, because I know the reality of what happened next. And it needs to be told.

All I can ask is that you resist the urge to rationalize or judge until you have read the whole story. Then please draw your conclusions freely.

Here goes...

13
THE SHATTERING

Have you ever walked into a room and had that creepy feeling like, "Whoa, what is *in* here?" Or can you remember ever awakening from a nightmare out of a dead sleep and experiencing the shock of overwhelming terror for no apparent physical reason?

That kind of suddenness describes how a quiet evening at home turned absolutely life-altering. That's no hyperbole, either, because how I viewed the world—spiritually or otherwise— would never be the same.

ço   ço   ço

It was nearing the later part of the evening. Life seemed to return to normalcy and total calm. Tyler and I cleaned up after dinner and were ready for our daily Bible reading when he said, "Look, Jess, we need to talk about what happened earlier."

Slightly embarrassed, I looked down at my hands. I knew that talking about it was a good thing, and I felt no apprehension about having the discussion. I didn't feel attacked or stressed because this wasn't the kind of thing Tyler and I would argue over. Talking about this subject meant working it out and learning from it.

Neither of us had even opened our mouths to speak when something changed. It was like a thundercloud rolled in out of nowhere and there was no time to run for cover. With sharp suddenness, an intense palpable hatred and a general sense of hideous evil absolutely overwhelmed me. The best I can explain it is this: Imagine the creepy, haunted-house feeling we just discussed. Combine that with the abrupt, nightmarish terror, then take that sensation and turn the intensity up as far as it goes, and that's the closest description I can give within the limitation of language. Evil and terror engulfed me. But having done as much work with energies as I had, I knew this was not just a feeling. This was something real—some*thing* real. Its essence was of terror and hate and evil. But here is the truly horrifying part: it did not come from somewhere on the outside, the way creepy feelings would if you walked into a spooky old house. Whatever it was clearly came from *inside me.* I could feel it welling up from deep in my belly, as though it were rolling into a dense ball that wanted to come up and out through my mouth.

The intensity of the rising shocked me like a sucker-punch. My eyes filled with terror and darted to meet Tyler's.

"Tyler…." My voice quivered at barely more than a whisper as fear dripped from my eyes in unblinking tears. "I don't know what is happening right now, but I'm getting super freaked out."

The gravity of my words and reaction must have silenced any questions Tyler had. Instantaneous fear showed in his wide-eyes and clutched him as he grabbed my hand. He knew something very real was happening, but like me, he had no idea what it was.

Petrified, I fixed my gaze forward, overwhelmed by what I can only describe as dark evil quite literally rising from inside me. Words are insufficient to describe the experience. The closest I can come is to say that a mass of self-hatred and hatred for everyone and everything else was combined with anger, rage, darkness, and pure, terrifying evil—and all of it was rising from my belly.

This was more than a feeling. It had an unmistakable *energy* to it, like when you feel nauseous and your body want to expel the "yuck"—there was something to vomit out. But this was more than physical; it was occurring, not at the level of matter, but of energy. In all of my energy work, I had never heard of or experienced anything like it. I was terrified, especially because it arrived out of nowhere and for no reason that was apparent in that moment.

As Tyler took my hand, I looked down, utterly consumed

by what welled up within me. Before I knew it, I felt myself lean slightly forward in my chair, over the table. My mouth opened ever so slightly as a barely audible but deep and throaty hiss spewed out from way back in my throat.

"What was that?" Tyler demanded, aghast.

"I don't know." My soft reply was almost pleading.

This was a terror more profound than any I could have imagined. I had not consciously chosen for my torso to lean over the table. Nor had I elected to form the throaty hiss that bared my teeth. It was not a noise I even knew how to make. It just happened.

Never had I heard of anything like this, or seen or read about anything that came close. So much was going on inside me. The dark feeling was getting stronger, like everything in me wanted to be consumed by it. As it rose from my belly, I felt my lips draw back slightly and bare my teeth as it moved up toward my face. A throaty hiss discharged from deep inside. There was almost a craving to be taken over by it.

Yet there was the split once again—the dichotomy I sensed on the other occasions—a calm, authoritative thought broke through the "noise," shot through my mind, and came out of my mouth. Before I was aware of what I was saying, three desperate words rang out: "Pray, Tyler. Pray!"

Then everything began to click as a flash flood of understanding rushed in. I cannot explain how, but in a matter of moments, years of what I had managed to deny made itself apparent.

I remembered my first choice to reject the Bible's teachings and work with mediums and spirits after Lela's passing. When I thought I was talking with Lela there had been that esoteric energy of blissful love and peace that convinced me the experience was good. The Bible never gave me that kind of physical validation, so I decided it had been corrupted by people and their agendas, and had not come from God. The

The Shattering

Bible said not to dabble in the spiritual realm because it was full of deception and lies. But I didn't want to believe that part.

The realization struck me. I gasped inwardly. It was true. The Bible was *all* true. Every single part I'd written off . . .

My thoughts raced with immediate comprehension in ways I cannot explain as the shocking reality of what was happening within me settled with a slam. The truth of it was undeniable. I had done enough work with energies and spirits to recognize their presence.

There was no rationalizing away what became so real to me at that moment—the dark, negative energy that was inside me. The intensity of it pulled me deeply and mercilessly. And, again, the dichotomy was present—the hate/evil/terror wanted to consume me; but something else was pushing it to come up and out of me.

I felt it rising in me higher and more intensely now. Oh, I wanted to vomit it out so much—a horrible, energetic vomit. The feeling was consuming, almost like I had to do it, like it was the only thing that mattered. It was getting stronger—all the evil feelings welling up, building and building. I was completely aware of my surroundings and of what was happening the whole time. I knew I was sitting at the table with Tyler; and I knew that if what was inside me came out in any form resembling what it felt like on the inside, I would likely lose Tyler forever.

How would any guy be able to stay with me after something like that? My brain was firing off possible outcomes like an automatic weapon sprays bullets. But future outcomes didn't matter anymore. The only thing that mattered was getting what was inside of me *out*.

Tyler prayed fervently to God. As the evil rose and consumed me, an authoritative thought shot through my mouth again with a quick desperation I had never felt. "Jesus," I practically gasped, surprised by my own words. "You have to use Jesus' name—*pray to Jesus.*"

"I was going to," Tyler said as he immediately switched his words. His face revealed an expression of hurt, as though I didn't believe he was praying to the right God. In retrospect, it wasn't that Tyler was wrong to address his prayer to God; it was just that I had associated so many things with the word *God* over the years that there had to be no mistake about the one to whom we prayed. It was through the name of Jesus that God conquered death and broke the chains of the dark spiritual realm. The power we needed was in his name.

The consuming energy of terror grew stronger and rose higher within me. The fact was not lost on me that this horrid thing was happening within a month of my telling all the other spirits I had ever worked with that I would from that point work only with Jesus. Nor was it a coincidence that this was happening right after my tearful realization of Jesus' suffering and death—and one day after reading aloud the story of his resurrection from the book of Luke.

What was rising within me was obvious; the reality of it was stark and undeniable. Just moments earlier, I would not have believed it was possible: I had allowed and even invited energies—spirits—of evil and darkness to come inside me.

The realization triggered a series of "Oh my gosh" moments. I knew in an instant why the Bible warns repeatedly against communicating with "the dead" or "spirits." I thought of the Bible verses I had chosen to ignore all those years, to the point that I had completely forgotten about them until that moment. The one about Satan himself masquerading as an angel of light haunted me.[9] I thought about my phase of working with "angels of light," and many, many other spirits.

The ancient Bible truths hit me, and I remembered all the "spiritual" things I had done in defiance of the Bible. My mind raced to register its new harsh reality. I recalled the myriad spiritual practices I had engaged in during the preceding ten years; and finally, the true forms of the energies were revealed. The evil inside me was plain. The energy was undeniable. It was rising from deep inside and it was coming out.

The Shattering

The hate/evil/and terror ball continued building to the point that I had no choice but to "vomit" vigorously. Weird and terrifying, it demanded my inward okay. It was much like the physical urge to vomit—while almost overpowering, I still had to *decide* to throw up, overwhelming as it seemed. When I did, my stomach contracted in the typical hurling motion. But instead of expelling physical matter, something spiritual was forced out. Rage and terror overwhelmed me and another ferocious, teeth-baring hiss lurched from deep in my being. I hissed and vomited all at once.

I felt absolutely consumed by evil. Yet, it felt good to let the evil come up and go out. I remember thinking that one more just left. But there was barely a moment's relief. It lasted only until I returned to a slouched sitting position before the next rising came.

This second expulsion was stronger than the first. My stomach contracted and lurched me forward as my arms drew backward. The teeth-baring and hissing were even more pronounced this time. An overwhelming urge—to form my hands into claws—gripped me. I fought it with everything in me so as to not freak out Tyler any more than I already had.

Even as I fought, I remained totally aware. Tyler was holding my hand and praying shakily. I knew it and was equally aware of what my body was doing. I heard the prayers, too. I was well aware of everything.

Instantly, my mind flashed to a crystal bowl meditation I had attended some years earlier. A woman from whom I had taken psychic development classes also offered a weekly meditation in which she would contact our guides and other "beings of light." She did this in order to learn which beautiful tones to play on her massive set of crystal bowls so that whatever healing, visions, or experiences we needed could be invoked. Every time she played the bowls, without fail, I quickly dropped into a deep meditative state. Each week, I had intense experiences of surging energy and visions.

I had also read about traditions involving spirit animals, and I was interested in what mine was. One week, as the psychic played the calming tones on her bowls, I felt deep waves of soothing energy flow through me as a vision came to mind. I was a black, panther-like creature. But it was more than a vision. The best way I can say it is this: I had the experience of physically *becoming* the catlike creature. It was me and I was it. I *felt* the slinky way it/I walked. I felt my hands become claws and felt what it was like to have claws. It was *exactly* like what was happening now: as I sat at the table, my hands longed and even ached to take the form of claws in the very same way.

Before every crystal bowl meditation I followed procedures so I would be completely protected from any negative energies. I did exactly as I was taught by experienced and respected teachers, so I was not troubled by the black panther experience at the time. I had simply wondered what my spirit animal was, and so I found out. There didn't seem to be anything creepy or even abnormal about it. The experience was accompanied by feelings of peace and love, and was not unlike other blissful and esoteric meditative experiences. I was used to working with energies and spirits, so this one was neither surprising nor bothersome.

None of my meditative and other spiritual experiences ever felt the least bit negative to me. If they had, I would have been terrified and stopped the practice immediately. Instead, every occurrence was accompanied by "loving energies." Peace and love were the only feelings I *ever felt*.

Everything I had been doing seemed fine—healthy and helpful, even. I was not interested or ever involved in anything dark. I never even watched scary movies. I dealt only in light. Now, however the truth was being revealed that darkness can effortlessly hide under a mask of beautiful light.

And in an instant, my reality was shattered.

14
DEPARTURES ON HOLD

Still at the table, I fought the urge to form my hands into claws. It was becoming more difficult to resist. It seemed like each spirit that arose within was stronger than the preceding one. Although I felt the release of something every time I vomited, I knew it was not over. I would return to a normal sitting position, have a moment to regroup, and then feel another one rising. Because the intensity kept increasing, I wasn't sure I could endure. Would the next one take over my physical body and form my hands into claws? The urge to let that happen was strong.

The uncertainty about the next one terrified me. Really, *terrified* is not a strong enough word. My mind whirled with the awful possibilities. Fear gripped me because everything I thought I understood about the spirit world and everything I had studied and worked with for ten years had been completely overturned in a matter of minutes. I thought I had all the rules of how the spiritual world operated pretty well squared away. But at that point I had no idea. The rug on which I'd been standing—the one my entire life paradigm had been built upon—was pulled out from under me. I no longer knew what I was standing on, or where, or how.

All I knew was that Tyler's prayers in Jesus' name felt like a powerful lifejacket wrapped around me. The name *Jesus* seemed to keep me in some level of protection and from drowning in the sea of darkness that was trying to consume me. On a spiritual level, I very much sensed that prayers in Jesus' name were the only thing keeping me from being controlled by the stuff that so desperately wanted to take me over.

At that moment, I trusted in only two things: the fact that there was safety in Jesus' name and the reality that every word of the Bible was true. The latter was a scary thing because I hardly knew what the Bible said anymore. But I no longer trusted anything else I'd learned since the psychic experience after Lela died. I clearly did not believe the rules of the spirit world as I had understood them up to that point.

Another thought terrified me: What about the things that were coming out of me? Could they stay around or come back in? Were they able to go into Tyler?

As I became overwhelmed with the fear of what might happen next, in my mind flashed a thought of going back to Don and Dawn's ranch. I had a feeling that if I got there, it wouldn't matter what came out or how strong it was. I knew I would be okay because Don and Dawn knew what the Bible said about all of this. I would be protected because, at the ranch, they worked only with Jesus. If I could just get there, I would be safe.

I took a deep breath and decided I would not let anything else come out, at least not that night. Immediately, the intensity of the evil and terror deflated like a balloon punctured by a pin. Though the terror and evil lessened, I knew they hadn't left, but only resettled deep within me. It was apparent that something even stronger than what had already come out was still inside me. Oh, how desperately I wanted everything out right then; but I was determined to wait until I got to the ranch.

It was late into the night by this time. I couldn't drive the five and a half hours now, especially as terrified as I was. I had no way of knowing whether the strong one still within me would rise up and take me over or try to run me off the road. I didn't know what I believed about *anything* at that point except for this: something very real inside me wanted to consume me. It wanted me dead, and I knew it. I don't know if you've ever felt such terror as I felt that night, but I can tell you that I had certainly not, nor have I on any occasion since, felt anything as awful.

The grip of hate/evil/terror decreased quickly once I made the choice to finish the process at the ranch. Within moments it was completely gone, as though it had been sucked up by a vacuum cleaner. Tyler and I sat in shock and stillness. I took a deep breath and finally, hesitantly, turned to Tyler, wondering what he thought about what had just taken place.

"Are they gone?" His words were quiet, but as intense as his facial expression.

I hadn't said anything to Tyler about what was happening within me. We had never talked about evil spirits or anything like that. Why would we have? But it was obvious what it was, even to him. What transpired was undeniable. He hadn't stopped clutching my hand or praying the whole time. I wanted to cry. I wanted so badly to be able to tell him they were gone—to at least ease the fear and apprehension I knew he must have felt.

But I couldn't lie to him. I shook my head and watched silent tears spill onto my lap.

"No," I managed. "No, there's one stronger. I have to go to the ranch. I know I need to go there and everything will be okay."

I paused, searching for the right words, not being able to even imagine the terror and confusion he must be feeling.

"I'm sorry...." I started to speak, but my words just hung there. They seemed so silly, so inadequate. "Tyler, I don't...I don't even know how to explain all of this. I've never experienced anything like it. I've never even *heard* of anything like this."

My eyes betrayed my desire to appear collected. Tears streamed down my cheeks, but my voice remained calm. I felt shaken up, but I no longer sensed the overwhelming presence of evil. It had totally disappeared, settled in some unknown space.

"Tyler, I would not want to stay in the same place with me tonight after seeing what you just saw. I understand. Really, I don't blame you at all."

I fumbled meekly, my mind struggling both to process what had happened and to consider the thoughts that must be swimming through Tyler's mind. "I'm…I'm going to get a hotel room tonight." I was calm and assured, although still in shock. "I'll just go for the night and leave for the ranch in the morning."

"No," Tyler shook his head with authority. "No, you're not going to a hotel. You're not going anywhere by yourself." He paused, apparently grasping for what the appropriate next move would be after the kind of events he had witnessed. "I'm…I'm going downstairs to just think for a little bit. I want you to sit here and pray to Jesus until I get back, okay? I do not want you to stop praying until I come back, do you understand?"

I nodded. It was what I had planned to do anyway. Just the thought of praying to Jesus brought me comfort. I prayed in a soft whisper the whole time Tyler was gone. It was a long, desperate prayer for Jesus to keep me safe—to save me from what I had opened myself up to when I turned my back on him. By the time Tyler came back, I was filled with peace—not the kind of physical, energetic, false peace I had encountered in the past, but a sense of deep, abiding tranquility.

Although I no longer felt even a trace of the evil energies, I knew at least one was still inside me. But Jesus was there, too. I didn't understand how that worked, but I knew he wouldn't leave me. I thanked him the way a drowning child thanks a lifeguard who pulled her out of the water—clinging to him with terrified, genuine, unabashed thankfulness.

Never had I known such gratitude as at that moment. I *knew* Jesus wouldn't leave me.

15
COMING TO TERMS

Tyler and I stayed up talking all night. But I was completely at peace the entire time. I continued praying in my head during pauses in our conversation. And when the conversation turned to the unpleasant subject of my past, the usually painful discussion was instead peaceful. The prayers were working on many levels. I felt completely protected and serene.

At around 6 A.M., we finally drifted off to sleep. I woke up four hours later and immediately called the ranch. There was no answer. I left a message and fell back asleep. We woke up again around one in the afternoon. This time when I called, Dawn answered and I explained the reason for my call. "Um, Dawn, it's Jessica. Um, something…something really, really scary happened last night and I, uh…I really feel like I need to come back there, if that's okay."

She asked if she could put Don on speakerphone and I did the same with Tyler. Then we shared what happened.

Much to my amazement, Don and Dawn were neither shocked nor surprised. They simply and calmly answered our questions. Dawn suggested that I go through the house and get rid of any books, statues, etc.—anything that represented anything I used to work with. It was important, Dawn said, that I state something to the effect of, "In the name of Jesus, you (stating the thing by name) have no power over me. I rebuke you (stating the name again) in the name of Jesus."

This wasn't an exercise in how to sound like a crazy, extremist Christian. It was actually important for me to clarify whose side I was on. I had to make my choice known, cut ties with the items and activities, and cease all engagement in the acts associated with each item. Every time I stated my choice, I was reminded that Jesus was stronger than whatever was associated with these things.

Expecting the process to be quick, I was surprised as I started going through my belongings—there was stuff everywhere. Some items were more obvious than others. There were many books, statues, and pictures of Buddha and Tara (a Buddhist deity I did a lot of work with). I also had photos of "saintly teachers" from India with whom I had felt an affinity, and to whom I had prayed for guidance.

Then there were the Tarot cards and angel cards through which I asked my guides and angels to communicate with me on occasion. I had crystals which I'd "programmed" with energies for different healings, and mala bracelets and necklaces I used to practice repetitive mantras that achieved a meditative state of openness and enabled me to access specific energies.[10] I had CDs of chanting and meditations, my reiki healing notes and certificates, astrological charts, and many, many more items.

Anything that had *anything* to do with communicating with anything spiritual, I threw away. It was clear to me that unless an item was shown in the Bible to be on the Lord's side, it needed to go.

The items I'd collected and used were deceptive, just as the Bible warns. Satan has the art of deception down. He is fully capable of making things look beautiful and good, totally unassuming, sweet, and even innocent and healthy. But the underlying reality is evil in its truest form. Ten years earlier, I didn't want to believe that; I didn't want to believe it even a month or days before. But at that point, I had no choice but to believe it. It had become impossible to deny.

I felt no attachment to anything I threw away, only loathing and repulsion—and the desire to rip things up so that no one would ever find them and fall into the traps that had ensnared me. Tyler and I disposed of boxes and boxes full of stuff. By the time we were done, it was dark.

❧   ❧   ❧

We had gotten a late start that day, so we decided that

I would stay one more night and leave for the ranch in the morning, alone. Part of me wanted Tyler to come along. But I didn't know what was going to happen at the ranch, and I never again wanted him to see me in the state he had witnessed the night before.

I didn't know what might happen or whether the "stronger one" that was still in me would exit in the same terrifying way, or worse. With so many unknowns, I thought better not to take the chance. Besides, I knew Tyler didn't want to see me like that again, either. He was struggling with what he'd already seen.

Who wouldn't have struggled with it? My going alone would give Tyler some time alone to play his music and get some rest. That's what he really wanted to do; I could tell he was exhausted. And surprisingly, he was sore. He said that as he held my hand and prayed, a very physical, intense cold passed through his legs. Afterward, his legs were very sore, as though they had been overworked. I understood that, because my own body was also sore.

I admit I was worried about driving by myself. Being alone in a car sounded scary because I no longer trusted my knowledge of the spirit world. In a very real way, I knew the spirits I used to work with were pure evil and wanted to kill me. They were also aware of my plan to visit the ranch. They knew the rules, and what would happen there. I had asked Don and Dawn whether we would be able—for certain—to get the spirits out. They assured me that any evil spirits *had to leave* in Jesus' name, because he has authority over all evil.

This brought an entirely new depth and reality to the idea that "Jesus saves." For the first time in a *really* long time, I wasn't annoyed by the expression. Instead, I was overwhelmingly grateful. Dawn said I would be fine; I was prayed for and I was protected. She suggested that I listen to Christian radio stations the whole way (which normally would have irritated me horribly). She also encouraged me to pray.

The thought that any evil spirit would love to scare me out

of my mind made me determined not to be afraid. I didn't want my actions or attitudes to give one more bit of satisfaction to any evil entity.

℘ ℘ ℘

The next day, I set out for the ranch. I had already planned to travel that direction for a yoga class I was scheduled to teach in a few days. I wanted to know whether all the evil spirits would be out in time for me to teach the class. I had no idea how all this worked. Maybe a recoup time was needed after something like this. Or maybe I could just return to my normal routine.

So I called Don and Dawn. When I mentioned my yoga class, I heard Don speaking in the background. Dawn relayed his message. "Jessica, Don really feels he must tell you that if you teach your yoga class on Saturday, your life will be in danger."

I really didn't see how that was possible. I certainly understood how the depths of "real" yoga had opened doorways to the stuff inside me. The yoga I had studied in India involved chanting mantras, which invites energies. It had just become very clear to me that praying to anyone besides God in Jesus' name was praying to an evil spirit that posed as something else. And praying to an evil spirit, however disguised as an energy or being of light or whatever, is *inviting* it.

In my mind, this class I was scheduled to teach was different from "real" yoga. It was a gym yoga class; it wasn't as "pure" as what I had been taught in India. I never incorporated chanting in my Saturday classes because it didn't seem appropriate. I was told that the owner wanted only the exercise part of yoga, not the spiritual part. So out of respect, I never even began or ended my classes by chanting "Om" (the chant that sets the intention to invoke Ishvara).

I had always thought omitting the chant was really sad because the potential depths of peace people could have reached through it and other mantras was lost. At that point, however, I was thankful that the owner hadn't wanted a "spiritual" class at her gym. I wondered whether I had opened any of my students to exploring the dangerous depths I had embraced, or if I had exposed them to anything that was spiritually harmful in any way. Yoga poses and breathing were the only things I taught them. The only "depths" we explored involved breathing techniques and relaxation, and sometimes guided meditations at the end. I didn't see how any of that would endanger me now.

The reality of yoga hadn't completely registered with me yet. But I no longer cared whether or not I understood the danger. I was in no position to claim any great wisdom. As much as I wanted to, I had not forgotten the fact that an evil spirit had risen in me during recent nights and had temporarily settled down inside me. So, if Don and Dawn said that I should not teach yoga, then I didn't need to.

Yoga was no longer important to me. So I called and canceled my class, adding that I would be unable to teach yoga in the future—ever.

16
BARING THE FOUNDATIONS

When I arrived at the ranch on Thursday evening, Don, Dawn, and I lingered over small talk for quite a while. I knew they were waiting for me to mention what had brought me there. Even though I wanted to tell them, a part of me wanted to hold off. It felt a bit like going to have a tooth pulled or a brand-new surgery; I knew it needed to be done, but so much was uncertain, and I dreaded the unknown. At the same time, it felt good to be in the living room where I knew I was safe. I wanted to savor the sense of relief a little longer.

As I broached the subject of the stuff that was inside me, Dawn asked whether I knew its name. One of the ways I had learned to communicate with the spiritual realm was to sit quietly and wait for the impression. It was kind of like using a Ouija board, but instead of the answer being spelled out on the board, it came in some form in my mind. So I sat quietly for a moment, waiting to see if anything would come up.

Then the unmistakable name *Bernadette* penetrated my thoughts, accompanied by a feeling of malicious spite. I knew the impression wasn't true, but I dutifully reported it. "It's saying, 'Bernadette.'"

Then came the next word. "Phillips." *Bernadette Phillips.* The name meant nothing to me. I just shrugged.

Dawn promptly brushed it off. "Oh, it's just messing with us. We won't give it the time of day. We don't need to know its name, and we won't talk with it."

Dawn moved on in the conversation. After a few sentences, in the middle of her speaking, a word arose in me and come out of my mouth. It arrived from out of nowhere and was spoken before I could process the fact that I was going to say anything.

"Serpent. Its name is Serpent."

My words surprised me, even though they were in my voice. They came out so fast and unexpectedly. I would never have thought of such a name. The way it came out shocked me—both the words I spoke and the way I interrupted Dawn mid-sentence.

Dawn just nodded. "Now, there's the truth," she commented. Then she moved on as though nothing had happened.

At one point, she asked me about yoga. She wasn't sure what it was or what it was about. I explained to her that the ultimate goal of yoga is not to tone the body, but to reach a meditative state in the mind and ultimately yoke one's consciousness with a type of godhead. This deity was called by many names including "the Divine," "the Universe," and others; but is encompassed by the sound of *Om*.

Driving to the ranch, I'd thought a lot about yoga. I realized it was best not to teach even my "gym yoga" class because it could lead someone to become interested in the tradition. Then they might decide to do some research and get into the same stuff I had gotten into. I did not want to encourage anyone along the deceptive spiritual path I had followed. I decided that there was nothing wrong with exercising the body by holding poses or going through a series of stretching movements. But it was not to be done in the context of a yoga class, because that is very assuredly *not* what yoga is, regardless of the claims made in gym yoga classes.

What do I mean? Yoga is a spiritual act aimed at "yoking" the practitioner with the spiritual realm. The word *yoga* is said to mean "yoke"; but many yogis have also translated it to mean "connect."[11] The practice yokes and connects the practitioner to the spiritual realm. Chanting uses the voice to invoke the spiritual realm; yoga uses the movement of the body. I was taught in multiple meditative traditions from Buddhism to yoga that intention is irrelevant. Whether you intend to invoke the spiritual realm by chanting or you chant only because you are following others in a class setting, the effect is the same. The act itself is the invocation.

So, if intent is irrelevant, what does this mean for the *poses* of yoga? One thing to consider is the historical evidence. It is well documented that many yoga poses are ancient acts of homage (or *worship*) to the gods associated with each pose or movement. We know that the act of yoga is to "yoke" with the spiritual realm. We have established that the invocation is not in the intent but in the act. What do you suppose this implies of the poses within the practice?

I repeat this because it is excruciatingly important: Although the goal of most Western practitioners is physical benefits, the goal of yoga (as it was taught to me in India and as it is recorded in countless traditional texts) is not primarily physical benefits. The physical outcomes are only a tiny sidebar. The main purpose of yoga is *spiritual* in nature. It is a **spirit-ual** practice.

Yoga, I explained to Dawn and Don, is essentially a movement meditation. The mind is focused and calmed through the pairing of the breath with the movement of the body. As I stressed that yoga is all about the breath, a shocking revelation hit me: Yoga is all about the breath.

When one learns yoga, he or she learns various breathing techniques. Just like with chanting, the "benefits" are received even without understanding what the techniques mean or how they work. Certain types of breathing bring sensations of peace and deepen the practice; that is what practitioners are taught.

Most anyone who has studied yoga in any depth is familiar with a breathing technique traditionally called *Ujjayi Breath* or *Breath of Fire*. It can be called different things in different schools of yoga, but the practice is the same. It usually takes a while for those just starting out to be introduced to this technique. Eventually, it is a goal of practitioners to use Ujjayi Breath throughout their practice (or to say it another way, throughout the entire yoga class).

Personally, I loved the technique because it brought a much

deeper level of meditative peace to my practice. Interestingly, you know you have the technique right when you hear a *low hissing sound*. We even told our students that.

When I was reminded of the hiss, something else struck me: yoga and many other spiritual traditions teach about an energy called *Kundalini* that lives at the base of the spine. In California, very early in my spiritual walk, I remember being guided in a meditation to access my Kundalini energy. It is taught that this energy can "awaken" and deepen one's spiritual practice. Yoga practice is one way to release this Kundalini energy.

Guess what the translation of *Kundalini* is? "Serpent."

I'm not one to draw overly-exaggerated conclusions. Typically, I want to see how "A" plus "B" equals "C," or I won't buy it. But these things are too uncanny not to at least point out. Perhaps it was sheer coincidence that the intense, throaty hissing that spewed out of me earlier that week was an exact, but super-intensified version of Ujjayi Breath. Maybe it's totally coincidental that Kundalini—believed across various spiritual traditions to be a primary energy "awakened" on one's spiritual journey—means "Serpent."

And maybe the fact that Satan appears as a deceiving serpent[12] is just one more coincidence. You can judge for yourself. All I know is that these facts struck me in a very strong and disturbing way.

After I explained some things about yoga, Dawn asked me to verbally list anything I could think of that I might have let in. I began with the obvious: Tara and Buddha. Then I listed some others. The exercise soon went the way typical of my spiritual experiences as information started coming out that I wasn't even thinking. Many thoughts flowed without the engagement of my conscious mind: the names of spiritual teachers; a couple of common names that didn't make sense to me; the one who called himself Archangel Michael (I had worked with him quite a few years earlier, but not in recent years); the angels Gabriel and Uriel (who I used to work with); reiki; and cocaine.

That last one surprised me. I would never have thought to mention drugs or to think that I had let in something evil by dabbling with drugs so many years prior. I went through a short-lived stage where I toyed with "party" drugs quite a bit. Then I did them more sporadically over a few years. I was fortunate never to be "addicted" (though I watched friends wither to skeletons, drop out of school, and sell all their possessions to keep on with their habits). When I finally realized how gross the drugs really were, how close I was to becoming addicted, and how horrible they really made me feel, I stopped. It had been many years since I had done any, or even thought about them. Further, I had never even tried any hallucinogenic drugs of any kind, and they were the only ones associated with "spiritual" experiences as far as I knew.

Then the face of a very prominent Buddhist leader and personal teacher appeared in my mind. For the life of me, I could not think of her name, which was interesting because I knew her and her name very well. It seemed like the image of her face was haunting me, and my memory was being blocked. After struggling to remember her name, I realized that I didn't need to know it.

That thought gave me peace. Calmly and confidently, I told Dawn what was happening. When I stated I would put the woman on the list without having to know her name, the image of her face (still fixed in my mind) twisted and contorted into a teeth-baring, monstrous-looking form. Then it vanished altogether.

Other items came up for the list, but I felt strongly that I had let in many more things than what I mentioned. I had opened myself to so much over the course of almost ten years that I would never be able to name them all. Dawn assured me that it didn't matter. She reminded me of the story in the Bible in which Jesus cast out legions of demons in one person.[13] He hadn't named them, but it didn't matter; all of them had to come out anyway. I think Dawn asked me about the names for my benefit. The exercise brought some surprises and helped me to understand in a very real way some of the ways in which evil spirits had gained entry.

It was getting late, so I made myself ask if we could go ahead and "pull the tooth." I didn't know what to expect, and I dreaded the thought of being consumed by that thing again. I never wanted to feel that sensation again.

I felt my lower lip tremble as I looked down at my hands and blinked back tears. Finally I admitted it: "I'm just . . . so . . . scared . . ."

Dawn replied with authority: "Jessica, you have nothing to fear. Absolutely nothing. They have to come out. They will come out. You are completely safe. Remember, they thrive on fear." Knowing how fear helped the other side gave me the jolt I needed to get out of fear. I decided I would not let the unwelcome squatters thrive—not anymore.

17
BREAKING FREE

Clueless as to what was next and not wanting to have any preset expectations, I told myself I would for once live by faith and not by feelings. The need for physical validation had gotten me into this mess in the first place.

I no longer knew the rules of the spiritual realm. Would the evil spirits leave in a similar manner as they had a couple of nights prior, or would it be completely different this time? Would it be more intense? Too powerful for me? Or would absolutely nothing happen?

Even though I really hoped there would be no noticeable manifestations, I knew it would be difficult for me to believe the spirits were gone if it seemed like nothing happened. But I told myself that I *would* believe it. There could be no hint of energy moving or leaving me whatsoever, and I would believe they were gone. I would have faith . . . finally.

I told myself that no matter what happened, I would say quiet little prayers to Jesus the whole time, prayerfully observing whatever occurred, even if it seemed as though nothing changed at all. I trusted that I was safe and that all the spirits would go. I would have no expectations—just observe, pray, and trust.

At this point, I felt completely at peace. Even while sitting on the couch and talking about all of this with Don and Dawn, I hadn't at all sensed any evil rising in me, so I figured it likely that nothing would take place. I would simply have to believe that the evil spirits were gone.

Dawn asked me to repeat a short Bible passage. Still feeling no trace of the terrifying darkness I had encountered two nights earlier, I felt completely normal. Then Dawn asked me to take a nice deep breath.

I inhaled deeply. Nothing happened. I exhaled slowly. Still

nothing. "Phew" I thought with relief. "Nothing is going to happen."

Even as I continued to exhale, I felt no trace of terror or evil, no hint of the energy that had previously overcome me. Throughout the exhalation, there was nothing.

Then, at just about the time when my exhale should have shifted into an inhale, it didn't. Instead, something started pushing my exhale further. Very slowly, my abdomen clenched tightly and drew my naval inward, leaning my upper body forward so that every last remnant of breath in my lungs was expelled. A low hiss escaped from the back of my throat. Even when the hiss came, I felt none of the terror that had accompanied it the last time. I returned to a normal sitting position, totally calm and peaceful. I continued to whisper little prayers to Jesus that kept repeating his name. I felt such safety in saying his name.

I had no idea whether another spirit was going to come out or whether anything else would occur. I reminded myself that I didn't need to know. I was satisfied in knowing that they had to leave, and I didn't need to know in that exact moment whether or not there were more to come. I just needed to pray quietly and confidently, accepting whatever transpired. Whether it took moments or all night, all the evil spirits would leave, and I was safe.

This was so different from the experience I had nights prior. I still felt the presence of pure evil that wanted to consume me as it arose within. Also remaining were the physical and emotional reactions. My stomach contracted; something I can best describe as pure hate manifested energetically, physically, and in a very real way; and my mouth opened in the same teeth-baring hiss.

The difference was that I no longer felt terrified. This time I didn't feel like I had to prevent the spirit from taking control of me. I could feel it wanting to overtake me, just like it did at my kitchen table earlier that week. But this time it had zero power to accomplish its desire. My prayers to Jesus—saying his name—infused a peace that I cannot explain.

I remembered the last time. Tyler held my hand and prayed for me, but I had been too consumed to pray for myself. Now, my own prayers to Jesus (and even just saying his name) carried such a transformative, authoritative power that I cannot describe it in words. Even though the evil I felt was very real, Jesus was clearly in control. The spirits *had* to leave. They had no power over me and no power in me.

Don and Dawn told me what the Bible says about when we decide to place our trust in Christ: God then places his seal of ownership on us.[14] This is his stamp, the mark that says we are his. Jesus had me. Dark energies could not have me any longer.

In a matter of moments, my body repeated the same motion in which my stomach contracted, leaning me forward in a vomiting motion while my teeth bared and a hiss came from my throat. I experienced an energetic release with each heave. It quite literally felt like I was vomiting out evil. I don't know how many times the pattern repeated. Nor could I physically see the spirits leaving. But the intensity and realness was blatant.

After each time, I came back to the sitting position totally at peace, and continued to pray. When the hiss would begin, my prayers went from a barely audible whisper to an inward expression. After the release of each spirit, I resumed praying.

At one point, it seemed like the pattern had been repeating many times. It may have been only a half hour or so; I'm not sure, because my sense of time was skewed. But I was so tired of it. It seemed as though the process would never end.

Would I ever know when all the evil energies were gone? Recognizing the fear, I quickly replaced the thoughts with hope and trust. Again I reminded myself that my lack of faith had gotten me into this mess to begin with. I would have faith now. They would all leave. It did not matter how long it took. I was safe. Period.

After each vomit, I sat back up at the edge of the couch and prayed. Sometimes only a moment would pass before another spirit arose; sometimes it was a matter of minutes. Don and Dawn calmly prayed and read the Bible aloud the whole time as though we were in a Bible study. Every so often as I prayed during a lull, Don would say something along the lines of, "Oh you will come out of her." Immediately, another vomit would happen.

At one point, my elbows bent and my hands lifted slightly into the air from my sides. I had not chosen to lift them, and was not consciously moving them. But I was not at all scared, either. I was simply an interested observer. My hands lifted to my sides and rotated lightly so that my palms faced upward. Then my thumbs joined my pointer fingers briefly. When they separated, my thumbs touched my middle fingers. These were the exact *mudras*, or hand postures, I almost always took during my peaceful meditations dedicated to love, light, and enlightenment for all beings.

Suddenly, my arms threw back and I violently hiss-vomited another release.

My body returned to sitting and praying. Right away, my upper body and my right arm began to move through a fluid, well-known yoga sequence. Like a lightbulb flashing, a word popped into my mind as the next hiss-vomit thing happened: *yoga*. Immediately, both arms thrust behind me with my chest pressed outward. Evil arose and spewed out in a teeth-baring, intense vomiting hiss. Then my body returned to sitting and praying.

Next my arms lifted with my elbows bent up and out to the sides, then pointed up to the sky. I had the feeling of wings; my back arched and my face looked upward, like my armpits wanted to be exposed to the sky. This was not painful, and I was still not scared. I was interested to see what this association was.

"Wings?" I wondered. "What is this one?"

I was at a loss. Then the lightbulb flashed again: *angels*. My arms had formed angel wings. They flew backward, my upper body heaved forward again, and another teeth-bearing hiss-vomit came.

I remembered that "Satan himself masquerades as an angel of light."[15] How had I never—not for one moment over the past ten years—allowed myself to seriously consider the possibility of truth in this statement? Had I really become so calloused to anything in the Bible that didn't fit my desired worldview that I had so completely forgotten about it? I had thoroughly written off such verses as examples of human error, the word of people instead of the Word of God.

The Bible clearly states that we are to worship God alone,[16] not his angels.[17] It says we should pray directly to God—*and no one else*—because we have direct access to him through Jesus Christ.[18] And it says that Satan is a deceiver, the "father of lies" and "a murderer from the beginning" who deals in disguises, deceptions, and death.[19] I finally understood.

The experience of breaking free was intense, yet I could have stopped what was taking place. It wasn't like something had taken total physical control of my body. I was fully aware and retained some control. For example, I felt I could have stopped my arms from lifting upward if I'd wanted to. I simply had a peace about the process and knew that Jesus was in ultimate control. I was not worried. So I let whatever was going to happen, happen.

Continuing to pray, still totally at peace and again sitting on the couch with my hands in my lap, I felt my body slide down to the floor. It was not my conscious thought to do this; it just happened. But again, I was not worried. I calmly prayed and observed.

As I slid to my knees, my upper body folded over until my forehead touched the ground and assumed yoga's resting child pose. I felt my arms slide forward along the ground until they were outstretched in front of me. My wrists bent so that my fingertips pointed up to the ceiling and my palms faced outward, parallel to the wall. I can describe it best as having felt like a releasing thought, about and through my palms. It made sense to me as I continued to pray. I felt a strong connection with my palms and with sending energy from my palms, exactly as I had done with all of my reiki and other healing energy work.

My torso raised back into a kneeling position and immediately threw my arms back as another hiss-vomit thing arose: *reiki*. I don't know how much time passed or how many more hiss-vomits there were in that kneeling position; but there were at least a few. Whether one spirit left during each round of retching, or many left each time, I cannot say. I am trying not to draw conclusions about things I don't know; and I don't know anything outside of what the Bible teaches.

At some point, nothing else was coming out. A peace settled, and we knew it was over.

18
AFTERMATH

So, that's the story of what happened. I told you it was intense. But it's true. And as hard as it is to tell it publically, I know in my heart that I must.

Already, I have shared it many times. People often ask me if I felt different after all of this. The answer is, "Yes and no." I was still the same person; but some things did change dramatically. The main thing I noticed was that I no longer felt repulsion for the name of Jesus. And, for the first time, I actually enjoyed listening to music that praised God. Not all of it—the sound of some of it still annoyed me, just like certain songs on any radio station would. But finally my dislike was about the particular sound of the music, not the lyrics that praised God.

Much to my surprise, I found that I actually wanted to listen to the music. That was really weird! I found a verse in the King James Version of the Bible that said God inhabits the praise of his people.[20] The use of the word *inhabits* sure sounds to me like where there is praise, there is God. No wonder it felt so good to have the music playing and to sing along with it! Now I love the music and it's all I listen to. There's some truly amazing Christian music out there today. (There probably always was.)

The only other difference I noticed was a new and almost overwhelming sensitivity to grossness, for lack of a better word. I just viewed things differently, I guess, without even trying to. Things that had never bothered me before—things I would have even enjoyed or thought funny, including certain jokes, words, or TV shows, etc.—suddenly repulsed me. I wanted to be as far away from that stuff as possible. This might sound strange, but they made me feel gross and defiled.

These are the main changes I can report. Over the course of some days, and seemingly out of nowhere, thoughts came up about things for which I needed to apologize to God. I had always rationalized them as being perfectly okay or even things to be proud of. Some involved people I had treated wrongly. None of it seemed like a big deal at the time, but it began to tug at my heart.

As for Tyler, I knew he wanted to be there for me. But he was not ready to let go of some unhealthy patterns that I knew could never be part of a healthy relationship. Immediately the old pattern of insistent, repeated discussions about my past reemerged, the details being rehashed over and over again.

I loved Tyler, but needed to move on from my past and accept who the Bible said I was: a new creation in the Lord.[21] I could not keep beating myself up; nor could I allow anyone else to do it. None of that stuff mattered anymore. And while I had been okay a month earlier with reading the Bible a little and taking from it what I wanted, I had changed; I longed to know exactly what it said—the whole thing. I wanted to live my life in accordance with Scripture, whether I liked what it said, and whether it was easy, or not.

Tyler thought this was too extreme. He liked the phase we'd entered before my second visit to the ranch, when neither of us felt the need to surrender *all* of our sinful habits. I wanted to follow the Bible. He wanted the Bible to fit into the choices he wanted to make. It wasn't going to work for us as a couple. Our foundations no longer matched. I loved him, and breaking up was excruciating; but I knew I could not go home with Tyler.

Part of the aftermath was the necessity of rebuilding my view of God and of all things spiritual. Really, I needed to rebuild everything, including how I wanted to live my life. I certainly did not want to hear anyone's opinions. Opinions had gotten me into trouble. The foundation of spiritualism and self-serving paradigms on which I had built my life and my sense of reality had crumbled beneath me. I didn't know what to believe, but I knew it wasn't other people's outlooks and ideas.

THE SHATTERING

What I needed was silence and time to process all that had happened. The only thing I knew was that I trusted what the Bible said, and I wanted to know every word of it. I didn't want to hear other people's interpretations of it or their views of what happened to me. I simply was not interested. I wanted to be alone with the Bible so I could study, pray, and come to my own conclusions.

I went home to my mom and stepdad's house and immersed myself in doing just that. My hands would search for my Bible before I opened my eyes each morning. I stopped reading only to eat and take care of other necessities of the day. After a while, I ventured out to the Christian coffee shop/bookstore downtown. There I read the Bible over chamomile tea and bran muffins, and recorded this story.

This experience has revealed to me many things that are clearly stated and supported in the Bible. I try not to read into things and draw any conclusions beyond that. I am certainly not saying that anyone who has meditated or done drugs or yoga has demons inside them. All I know is that those practices were named right before I vomited out spirits of pure evil. So do with this information what you want.

I am also not saying that anyone who has evil spirits inside them has to feel them leave in a physical way or any way that is similar to what I experienced. I don't know why this happened to me in this manner, except for the fact that there's no way I would *ever—**ever**—*have believed that my peaceful and loving work, including my healing work and my yoga practice, was actually darkness. No one could have convinced me of this, no matter what they said, had I not experienced what I did.

One thing I must say is that after everything I have been through, after examining every doubt and personal conviction in my heart and mind, I know the Bible explains exactly what happened and why. I know that to many of you, the possibility

The Aftermath

that the Bible is true is the craziest part of this whole story. But the more I read and research it, the more everything fits together—simply and amazingly.

You already know what I used to think—that it was ridiculous for anyone to believe the Bible. But once actually researched, the accuracy of the book defies the imagination. All the books of the Bible weave together like an intricate tapestry. The flawlessness with which every single predicted event has come true (exactly as revealed many years prior) is beyond any human conception of probability. These prophecies continue to unfold with precise accuracy even in current times.

This is a matter of documented, historical fact. The biblical prophecies and the reality of their coming true the way they have is mind-boggling. Believe me, I totally get the doubt about this because for many, many years I was the strongest *dis*believer in the Bible. I proposed that it was just a government method to control people. At best, I thought it remotely possible that the Bible was a cute way for gullible people to live happier lives. But now I am absolutely convinced that every word of the Bible is there because God wants it there, he inspired its inclusion, and he has a purpose and a plan for its being there.

I believe it is a dangerous practice to question the legitimacy of any part of the Bible the way I did, because it did not make sense to me or go along with my ideas of fairness or of how things should be. God's ways are higher than ours. I no longer need proof of that. I no longer need to stand with my hands on my hips, demanding to know why he chooses to reveal some things and keep others secret, or why he makes rules that seem to disagree with the culture or with what I might feel like doing at the moment.

I think about where I started to slip, and about how I went from the little girl who loved God to a young woman who despised the name of Jesus. My slippery slope began the moment I chose to ignore the little things I knew in my heart were right, and instead opted continually to do as I pleased. One small, rebellious choice at a time, I numbed myself to the voice inside that laid a finger on my guilt. I knew I shouldn't lie to my parents when I wanted to go to the party and stay out late. So I pushed the guilt away and did what I wanted: to drink beer because everyone else was doing it. I pretended that there was no nagging feeling telling me I shouldn't. I cracked open a beer (or maybe five) anyway.

Over the years, little by little, the awareness of guilt finally went away, and I gradually became numb to my once deeply-rooted morals. But it was when I determined that not everything in the Bible was true, that just one little section here or there must have been a mistake because it didn't fit the way I wanted life to look—that was when I greased the slippery slope and served up my own detriment.

I realize this could be the craziest thing you have ever read outside of fiction or weird, spam e-mail. It's certainly not something I ever planned to write. And I'm sorry if it causes you to feel as creeped out as I sometimes did living it.

Please know that I don't feel badly or uncomfortable talking about any of this. So I welcome your writing me at jess.ahner.smith@gmail.com to ask any questions you might have, even if you think they might seem disbelieving or offensive. I will do my best to reply. As I said, my own mind was as disbelieving and offensive as could be. But the truth beat out my best arguments.

19
REALITY IN A NUTSHELL

If you are reading this, you are likely interested in spiritual reality. I spent a long time seeking it before finally discovering the intense deceptions, and unearthing that everything is explained perfectly and mind-blowingly . . . in a single book. What was the point of this life? Why is this world the way it is? It explains all of that, too.

This is the most important part of the story: reality, as defined and explained in the Bible—in a nutshell.

Old Testament shows us how sin entered the world (humans chose to disobey God's instruction, thereby separating us from our relationship and eternity with him), how we repeatedly sin (this sin nature has been passed down to every human since), and how there is nothing we can possibly do to make up for our sinful nature (the penalty of sin is death). This means our sin separates us from a right relationship with God on earth, then our physical death separates us from God for eternity. But God had a plan. He let his people know that a perfect sacrifice could pay the penalty of death in our place, exemplifying this through instituting the sacrifice of unblemished animals (including lambs). But that wasn't the ultimate plan—he was only painting a picture of the gruesomeness of sin and the terribleness of its penalty that would be ingrained in the minds of his people. Animal sacrifices, no matter how flawless, could never pay our penalty in full because they are not a perfect substitute to take our place—they are not a "human" replacement. So the ultimate pure, perfect, unblemished sacrifice had to be human. But we all have that sin nature. No one but God is perfect. This allowed only one option for the restoration and salvation of humans: he had to send himself—an "extension" of himself—in the form of a perfect sacrifice. Because this concept is way too difficult for us to grasp, he calls this extension of himself something we can relate to: his one and only Son.

God would come to Earth as Jesus, the only perfect sacrifice, once and for all, to save anyone and everyone who turns to him from the consequence of sin, which is eternal darkness and death. (It is prophesied, by the way, that he will come again, but this time with a different purpose.) It is amazing that God predicted this in numerous places throughout the Old Testament, which was written long before it ever happened. Then thousands of years later (or hundreds depending on which prophecy you reference), he came and fulfilled every detail exactly as it had been foretold. I encourage you to look into the legitimacy of the recorded dates of these prophecies, and the odds of every single one of them coming true. (I highly recommend Lee Strobel's investigative work, *The Case for Christ*[22]—work he started as an atheist.)

Jesus came so that he could pay the penalty that we deserve, but in order to accept the gift and be saved, we must first display faith. If someone hands us a gift, we must receive it in order to possess it. God is offering the most amazing gift through Jesus, but we have to accept it by trusting that he actually has this gift to give—that he is who he says he is. We have to take a step of faith. God illustrates in story after story throughout the Old Testament that he requires his people to believe *before* they are saved and *before* he reveals his mighty miracles. He required Joshua to take a step into the river prior to parting it. He required them to march around a fortified city named Jericho for days, and blow horns on the seventh day, before the Lord supernaturally brought down the walls for them. He required Moses to approach Pharaoh, the powerful Egyptian ruler, and demand that he free all the Israelites. Only after that did God intervene with miraculous interventions that persuaded Pharaoh to let the people of Israel go.

When the people were led away from Egypt through the desert, they soon forgot the goodness and provision of the Lord and started complaining against Moses and the Lord that life wasn't good enough. To help the people realize they were wrong and should turn from their complaining, the Lord sent a wake-up call: venomous snakes—a vivid picture of the result of sin, which is always death (through poisonous serpents, no less). They quickly realized God was right; they apologized and repented, and they understood that only the Lord could save them.

They then asked Moses to pray to the Lord to remove the snakes. God offered them a way out, but it was not exactly the way they asked. God told Moses to form a bronze snake, put it on a pole, hold it up, and have the people look up at it. God didn't make the snakes vanish, just as he hasn't removed Satan or the sting of our sin. But he offered to neutralize the venom. All he required was for the people to *believe* enough to look up at the bronze snake. If they did, the lethal bite would not kill them. They would be saved by believing.

"What?" you may ask.

Exactly. It likely makes no sense to our minds. But whether we understand it or not, that is how God chose to do it. Those who chose to look up were saved from the deadly venom. By the same token, all who scoffed and refused God's offer died of the snakebite. It didn't matter if they were thought to be really good and nice people, or if they thought the whole thing was ridiculous. Regardless of whether they understood it or not, all that mattered was faith. That's the way it is with God. His purposes are so much higher than we can comprehend. We don't have to understand. We simply have to look to him and believe that he is faithful to his Word.

Centuries later, as predicted, Jesus came on the scene. When he healed people, he often told them, "Your faith has made you well."[23] He said this repeatedly. It was not their love, niceness, obedience, generosity, or their patience. It was their faith. Jesus hammered this point throughout his earthly ministry: *you must have faith to be saved.*

A Simple Offer

The Bible tells us that if we choose not to acknowledge that God sent his only Son, Jesus, (who died and rose again on the third day to save those who believe in him), then we are not his, and we are not saved from darkness and its power. But if we do choose to believe that his Son Jesus came and died for us, we are saved and his seal is stamped on us.[24]

It sounds so ridiculously simple; yet there is no in-between. John 3:16 clearly states "that whoever believes in him shall not perish but have eternal life." The Bible says our *choosing to believe* is the only way.

Jesus himself said, "I am the way and the truth and the life. No one comes to the Father except through me."[25] I don't know the reasons for this, but I do know that the more I study the Old and New Testaments in the Bible, the more his truth makes sense, and the more examples I find of God requiring faith from his people. He has done this from the beginning; it is only through having faith that people are saved.[26]

For whatever reason, this is his plan, and I have learned the hard way that it is best not to cross my arms, stomp my feet, and demand to know why. All I need to do is trust and believe him—and only him.

I used to believe that all "gods" were ultimately one, all connected to the same "Universe," or the "divine." But (as unpopular as it is to say this), any person who prays to anyone or anything besides the God of the Bible, through his Son Jesus, be it a god or an angel or a spirit of a living or dead person or being, is praying to a demon. This is not my opinion. This is the teaching of the Bible and it has definitely been evidenced in my life (see 1 Corinthians 10:19-20).

If saying this offends you, I am sorry. If I had read these sentences a few years ago, I would have slammed the book shut and thrown it away. But this is not some new thing I am making up—the Bible gives *so many* repeated warnings against praying to and dabbling with other gods or spirits. I share them only out of love for those who might be into the same practices I was, and also to anyone who may not have necessarily been involved in the exact same things, but who might pray to angels or the spirits of people who have died—to anyone but the Lord God through Jesus Christ.

Believe what you will, but it is my obligation to warn you: Please don't let supernatural experiences and the warm, fuzzy feelings of peace or waves of bliss that you feel during your prayers, meditation, or other spiritual practices deceive you. These are physical feelings and experiences that are counterfeited to trick you. Satan is fully capable of deception that goes beyond human comprehension.

Even if you think this all sounds exaggerated and extreme (or even too simplistic), the fact remains that according to the Bible there is one way—only *one* way—to be saved from this deception: Romans 10:9 says that "If you declare with your mouth, 'Jesus is Lord,' and believe in your heart that God raised him from the dead, you will be saved."

If you are struggling with what you have just read, but want to know and believe the truth, ask the Lord to help you. Faith is a gift.[27] If you don't have it and you want it, you can ask him for it, and he will give it to you in his perfect timing.

The Experiment

If you are honestly seeking truth and believe you have found it in any of the meditative practices (Buddhism, reiki, yoga, etc.)—practices that make you feel so lovely and peaceful that you cannot even imagine how darkness could be associated with them—may I propose an experiment?

For three months, give Jesus' path a go. He is a master of light, love, and healing, so what do you have to lose? Tell the Lord you want to know whether what I am saying is true. More important, you want to know whether what he is saying in the

Bible is true. Is Jesus the only way? Are the peaceful effects of these other practices really deceptions of Satan? If you are a sincere truth-seeker, then tell the Lord that you are. With your honest, truth-seeking heart let him know that you want the truth and are willing to accept whatever that is.

If you accept this challenge for three months (or longer, if you choose, but for three months, at least), you will give Jesus and the Bible an honest hearing. You'll also make a wholehearted effort to seek Jesus' path. This means you will cut out any and all practice—any prayers, chanting, classes (yup, even "gym yoga" classes); and you will put away any reminders of these practices (statues, mala beads, tarot cards, certificates, etc.), purposing to pray only to Jesus.

Ask Jesus to help you with this. Make it a priority to pray to Jesus or the Father in Jesus' name (as they are one and the same), even if it's only a little bit every day. Talk to him openly about your life and struggles. Ask for help, understanding, or anything else you want. He is your Father who loves you more than any of us can ever understand. He loves it when you spend time with him.

The last piece of the experiment is to learn and really understand what Jesus said and who he is. Four New Testament books tell the story of his life on Earth: Matthew, Mark, Luke, and John. As you read from one or all of them you will probably find some surprises. I know I was amazed at what Jesus actually taught as opposed to what people generally think about him.

The rest of the Bible is awesome, too. I recommend that you ask Jesus if he would like you to read anywhere else. See if you are drawn to any of the other books in it. Ask him to reveal himself to you through them. This book is his message to us; he wants to reveal himself.

The Bible is an amazing book. The Lord claims it is all from him, it is the only truth, and it is a complete work. There are many Bible translations available, as you might already know. I like the New International Version (NIV) because it's easier for me to understand; but other translations are good, too.

If you're anything like me, you have committed at some point to a period of time to try out a new diet or workout plan. How much more important is it to discover the truth about eternity than to find another way to sculpt our temporary bodies? What is three months out of an entire lifetime (and eternity, really)? How valuable is it to set aside any anger and resentment toward Christianity if it means learning about the path of the one whose ultimate teaching is the love of God and the love of others?

I trust he will reveal truth to you. I will be praying for you. Please . . . ask yourself what you have to lose.

Parting Thoughts

Finally, I encourage you, if there is any stirring in your heart or unsettled feeling about any of this: please do not ignore it. I recommend that you find a pastor of a Christian church to talk to. I know there are churches that call themselves Christian but are actually leading people astray. Some leaders' personal lives and preaching are also contrary to the Bible. But there are many great churches out there. I particularly like Calvary Chapel churches because they preach straight through the Bible, verse by verse, and cover it all—nothing more, and nothing less.

It is not the opinions and interpretations of others, but only the Bible that speaks truth. That's why it is of paramount importance that you read it yourself. Wherever you go, make sure the words you hear preached are backed up in biblical Scripture, and biblical Scripture only. I strongly urge you to check it for yourself. If you ask the Lord for guidance in truth and check the Scriptures for yourself, you should find it easy to discern which churches are real and which are fake-outs.

If you ever have (or had) a bad experience with a church, please, please, don't blame God for it. God is perfect. People are not. Please try again. Good churches are out there, I promise.

There are many reasons why it's important to get together with other people who believe, and not just watch a sermon on television and call it good.

For believers, gathering with other believers in fellowship is important. It builds them up and keeps them strong; and God commands his people to do it.[28] Those who believe Jesus is their Lord and Savior are part of his body—the body of Christ. Just as human body parts need the other parts to function properly, so believers need each other.[29]

If you would like the Lord in your life right now, the next chapter, "Salvation 101," has more information about what that means. If you are already a Christian, you are welcome to skip over to Chapter 21.

Thank you for spending part of your life reading about how the Lord worked his amazingness in mine. I pray he touches your heart through it, and continues to lead you to himself as you seek truth.

Allow me to leave you with a brief passage that I love because it is the gospel in a nutshell, straight from the mouth of Jesus.

> Just as Moses lifted up the snake in the wilderness, so the Son of Man must be lifted up, that everyone who believes may have eternal life in him. For God so loved the world that he gave his one and only Son, that whoever believes in him shall not perish but have eternal life. For God did not send his Son into the world to condemn the world, but to save the world through him. Whoever believes in him is not condemned, but whoever does not believe stands condemned already because they have not believed in the name of God's one and only Son. This is the verdict: Light has come into the world, but people loved darkness instead of light because their deeds were evil. Everyone who does evil hates the light, and will not come into the light for fear that their deeds will be exposed. But whoever lives by the truth comes into the light, so that it may be seen plainly that what they have done has been done in the sight of God (John 3:14–21).

THE SHATTERING

Part 2:
The Resource Room

20
SALVATION 101

This resource is for readers who want to have Jesus in their lives today. It's really simple, but I don't want you to simply take my word for it. Since it is always best to see what the Bible says, I listed some verses that outline specific truths of the gospel. *Gospel* means "good news." It is the story of why we need Jesus and how we can be saved by him.

THE LORD IS THE CREATOR, AND PEOPLE ARE WITHOUT EXCUSE

Romans 1:20

For since the creation of the world God's invisible qualities—his eternal power and divine nature—have been clearly seen, being understood from what has been made, so that people are without excuse.

EVERY ONE OF US HAS SINNED

Romans 3:23–24

For all have sinned and fall short of the glory of God, and all are justified freely by his grace through the redemption that came by Christ Jesus.

ALL HAVE TURNED AWAY FROM HIM

Romans 3:10–12

There is no one righteous, not even one; there is no one who understands; there is no one who seeks God. All have turned away, they have together become worthless; there is no one who does good, not even one.

THE RESULT OF SIN IS DEATH

Romans 6:23

For the wages of sin is death, but the gift of God is eternal life in Christ Jesus our Lord.

CHRIST DIED FOR US SO WE COULD BE SAVED
Romans 5:8
But God demonstrates his own love for us in this: While we were still sinners, Christ died for us.

John 3:16
For God so loved the world that he gave his one and only Son, that whoever believes in him shall not perish but have eternal life.

SALVATION COMES BY FAITH
Romans 1:17–20
For in the gospel the righteousness of God is revealed—a righteousness that is by faith from first to last, just as it is written: "The righteous will live by faith."

TRUST IN JESUS
Romans 10:9, 10, 13
If you declare with your mouth, "Jesus is Lord," and believe in your heart that God raised him from the dead, you will be saved. For it is with your heart that you believe and are justified, and it is with your mouth that you profess your faith and are saved....for, "Everyone who calls upon the name of the Lord will be saved."

REPENT
To repent simply means to confess to God and turn away from what you know is sin, and do your best to follow him.

Acts 3:19
Repent, then, and turn to God, so that your sins may be wiped out, that times of refreshing may come from the Lord....

PRAY
If you would like to pray today to be on the Lord's side, I encourage you to pray the prayer below. If you'd like to sign your name, go for it. It will be a sweet keepsake of the day your darkness turned to light.

Dear Father in heaven, I believe your Word and I want to believe more. Please give me more faith, Lord. I know I am a sinner. Please, Lord, I ask you to forgive me for all the wrong things I've done in my life. I trust your Word. I believe that you sent Jesus, your Son, as an extension of yourself to die for our sins. You are the Father, the Son Jesus, and the Holy Spirit, and I trust that only by having faith in you can I be saved. Please free me and protect me from evil. Please grow me in understanding, in your wisdom. I choose to turn from the things in my life that are not right in your eyes. I ask for your help. Please help me to live a life pleasing to you; please restore peace and joy in my life. I put my whole trust in you and ask that you come into my heart, Lord. Put your seal on me. Renew me, protect me, and grow me. Thank you, Jesus, for hearing my prayer. Thank you for saving me.

Signed_____ Date_____

I am so excited for you and for the way the Lord will now work in your life, if you let him. He restores all the areas of life we willingly surrender to him. With him, life can become so rich. This sincere choice keeps you for eternity, and that is awesome! But for *this* life to be rich, full of joy, and free from the oppression of evil—and to store richness in heaven for later—I encourage you to seek him daily.

God's Advice: Suit Up

I was amazed when I discovered the Bible passage listed below. In it, God tells us that the reality, whether we acknowledge it or not, is that we are involved in an ongoing battle in the spiritual realm.

Ephesians 6:10–12
Finally, be strong in the Lord and in his mighty power. Put on the full armor of God, so that you can take your stand against the devil's schemes. For our struggle is not against flesh and blood, but against the rulers, against the

authorities, against the powers of this dark world and against the spiritual forces of evil in the heavenly realms.

I love that the Lord doesn't tell us we are in very real battle with evil forces and then leave us to figure out how to fight it. Being the ever-sweet Father that he is, he gives us instructions to keep us protected and strong, and he tells us how to be his mighty warriors:

Ephesians 6:13–17
Therefore put on the full armor of God, so that when the day of evil comes, you may be able to stand your ground, and after you have done everything, to stand. Stand firm then, with the belt of truth buckled around your waist, with the breastplate of righteousness in place, and with your feet fitted with the readiness that comes from the gospel of peace. In addition to all this, take up the shield of faith, with which you can extinguish all the flaming arrows of the evil one. Take the helmet of salvation and the sword of the Spirit, which is the word of God.

How does that apply to our lives?

- *Truth* is the belt holding everything up. We must remember to be unashamed and remain unshaken when standing in the Lord's truth, no matter what we may feel or what society pushes us to think or feel.

- *Righteousness* is the breastplate protecting our most vital organ—the heart. When we disobey the Lord's commands, we give the enemy a stronghold, a hole in our breastplate of righteousness. But when we follow the Lord's instructions for living as instructed in his Word, our armor is strong and intact.

- *The Gospel of Peace* provides readiness that is fitted on our feet. This is the story of Jesus, the power of salvation. We are to know it so well that it carries us everywhere we go, and are ready whenever the Lord presents an opportunity to share his truth.

- *Faith* is our shield. The Bible says we cannot please God without faith.[30] We choose to believe, even when darts of doubt attack us. Fiery darts from the enemy will come in many forms. Satan knows that during trials, our natural tendency is to doubt. He depends on this tendency to tear us down. But if we repel the darts of trials and doubt by choosing to trust the Lord even when we don't understand or cannot feel him or sense his presence, we will be untouched. The Lord requires and rewards faith.

- *Salvation* is the helmet, protecting our head. It's a big deal, and we absolutely must have it. Salvation is received only by accepting the gift that Jesus came to offer us: eternal life through faith in him. If we truly place our whole trust in him, we will surrender to him by asking him to come into our lives. We then seek his will and a relationship with him, and do our best to follow him. This is not to say that we are by any means perfect. Nor does it mean that we're not saved if we sin (everyone sins). Following Jesus simply means that we have switched sides. We're taking our instructions from a different coach. The Bible says even the demons believe Jesus is the Son of God, yet they certainly are not saved. Salvation is more than belief. It is surrendering control (which is awesome, because God does a way better job of guiding our lives than we do) and following him.

- *The Word of God* is our sword of the Spirit. When Jesus was tempted by Satan in the wilderness and the fiery darts of attack came, he outfitted himself with the complete armor we are discussing now for protection. But Jesus used the sword of Scripture to cut Satan down. He simply spoke the Word of God by saying, "It is written . . . ," and quoting particular verses from the Bible. We must know what the Bible says and be ready to respond with it. The Bible declares in Hebrews 4:12 that the Word is living, active, and sharper than a two-edged sword.

What Now? (Some Web Resources)

Following Christ is a continual growth process, and the right resources can help our spiritual development. The first link I have listed is for a website from Pastor Greg Laurie. It is an excellent resource for new believers, with helpful insights into what happens next: http://www.harvest.org/knowgod/new-believer/start-to-follow.html.

Pastor Jon Courson's website is an awesome tool for Bible study. Over the course of many years, he has recorded and cataloged teachings of the entire Bible. You can search his digital messages (free of charge) either by topic or by the particular Bible verse or passage you are interested in. His teachings are awesome and the site is amazing! Here's the link: www.joncourson.com.

Another fantastic resource for solid teaching is Pastor Matt Fox's website at www.waylifetruth.org. He has also taught through the entire Bible, and made his teachings available. You can either download individual teachings totally free of charge, or order a complete set of teachings from Genesis through Revelation on MP3 (there is a price for MP3s to cover costs). Recent video services and radio programs are also posted. There is nothing like having access to accurate, in-depth teachings on every chapter of the Bible. I highly recommend it.

There are many good churches, and some that aren't so good. As already mentioned, I like Calvary Chapels because the denomination was founded to keep it simple and teach straight through every word of the Bible. Since knowing the entire Bible is so crucial to spiritual health and development, I'm a fan. Locating a Calvary Chapel in your area is easy. Just go to: www. calvarychapelassociation.com/churches/.

Remember: wherever you go to church, check out the Scriptures for yourself and pray. The Lord will guide you!

One more link: I already told you I would love to hear from you. Your questions are welcomed; and if you would like to share your decision for Christ, please e-mail me at jess.ahner. smith@gmail.com. I've been praying that the Lord would grow, protect, strengthen, and nurture you in your walk with him. I would be thrilled to hear how he is working in your life!

"For you were once darkness, but now you are light in the Lord. Live as children of light" (Ephesians 5:8).

21
THE LORD'S TAKE ON SPIRITUALISM

Without consciously realizing it, we can ignore and even deny God's warnings. Satan has a way of making things appear harmless, even fun and amusing. Perhaps it is a fortune teller at the fair, a woman who reads Tarot cards at Saturday market, or a silly "game" called the Ouija board. Maybe it is talking to a recently deceased relative or praying to a dead saintly teacher or an angel. While these things may seem like positive practices to some, it is my obligation to point out that the Lord of the Bible has a very different opinion. He knows all things, and takes this subject very seriously because its deception destroys his people. In order to protect us, he repeatedly sounds this alarm throughout the Bible: Never, ever consult mediums or attempt to communicate with any person who has died.

I discovered that there are many verses warning against this kind of activity. Here are three from the book of Leviticus:

Leviticus 19:26, 31; 20:6 (NIV)
Do not practice divination or sorcery.

Do not turn to mediums or seek out spiritists, for you will be defiled by them. I am the LORD your God.

I will set my face against the person who turns to mediums and spiritists to prostitute himself by following them.

Why would God refer to such dabbling in the spiritual realm as prostitution? How would we be defiled by asking someone to communicate with the spirit realm?

Here is what I have learned: it is better to believe God

first than to find out years later (as I did) how horribly we and others can be defiled by unbiblical spiritual practices. Though they may seem innocent, appear to be miraculous, and produce sensations of love and peace, they are well-crafted counterfeits. Such feelings and esoteric experiences can be easily conjured and manipulated by spirits that are definitely not on God's side.

When I thought I was talking to my deceased friend Lela (see Chapter 2), I was actually communicating with an evil spirit. Here is one of many verses that clearly shows it is against God's will to practice *divination*, which means to divine or to communicate with spirits.

1 Samuel 15:23
Rebellion is like the sin of divination, and arrogance like the evil of idolatry.

God provides two good reasons why he doesn't want his people going near these practices dealing with the spiritual realm. First of all, he says it is all a lie:

Zechariah 10:2
The idols speak deceitfully, diviners see visions that lie; they tell dreams that are false, they give comfort in vain. Therefore the people wander like sheep oppressed for lack of a shepherd.

God also explains in numerous places that such spiritual experiences are not what they appear to be, because demons are behind them.

1 Corinthians 10:20–21
The sacrifices of pagans are offered to demons, not to God, and I do not want you to be participants with demons. You cannot drink the cup of the Lord and the cup of demons too; you cannot have a part in both the Lord's table and the table of demons.

Psalms 106:36-38
They worshiped their idols, which became a snare to them. They sacrificed their sons and their daughters to false gods. They shed innocent blood, the blood of their sons and daughters, whom they sacrificed to the idols of Canaan, and the land was desecrated by their blood.

Deuteronomy 32:17
They sacrificed to false gods, which are not God—gods they had not known, gods that recently appeared, gods your ancestors did not fear.

Now let's get back to the idea that meditative practices, divination, sorcery, and other unbiblical spiritual experiences are not what they appear to be:

2 Corinthians 11:14-15
Satan himself masquerades as an angel of light. It is not surprising, then, if his servants also masquerade as servants of righteousness. Their end will be what their actions deserve.

If I had known and believed in my early twenties what I do now, I would have fallen to my knees in prayer and read every verse in the Bible that mentioned the spiritual world and how we should react to it. I would have devoured every verse I could get my hands on. Out of desperation, that is exactly what I did years later.

I could fill many pages with all the references on this subject. But I urge you to not simply take my word for it. Read the Bible yourself so you understand the context of the verses and passages I have listed. And even if you don't believe in him, ask God if he is real to reveal his truth as you read. He will do it. Desiring to know truth and asking God for it seem to be keys to understanding the Bible.

One more passage before we move on; this one does a good job of summing up the stance of the Lord, the God of the Bible, as it relates to the issue we are discussing:

Deuteronomy 18:10–12
Let no one be found among you who . . . practices divination or sorcery, interprets omens, engages in witchcraft, or casts spells, or who is a medium or spiritist or who consults the dead. Anyone who does these things is detestable to the Lord.

22
A NOTE TO CHRISTIANS ON YOGA AND MEDITATION

Here I want to address the subject of yoga and meditation from the perspective of those who follow the Lord Jesus. Please know that the following is shared out of love and not judgment. I, of all people, know how deceptive these practices can be. I write this not to chastise or beat up on anyone, but because you deserve to know the truth. (You can find additional information at: www.truthbehindyoga.com.)

YOGA

Yoga and a new, eastern definition of meditation are becoming very attractive and popular in our culture today. By nature, we human beings want to fit in and go with the flow. I understand that. And I would guess that many of you who practice yoga or relaxation meditation techniques might rationalize that these practices are okay because your type is not spiritual or is different from the more overtly spiritual forms I talk about. But I assure you, all forms of yoga are spiritual, and all have spiritual effects

In our society, yoga has been cleverly masked, being presented in one of two ways: (1) as a non-spiritual, exercise-only class, or (2) as a practice that retains spiritual aspects that are open to all religions.

In the latter example, Christian practitioners are encouraged to continue in their practices and simply "plug in" the God of the Bible. As an ex-yoga teacher who trained in India before becoming a Christian, I can tell you that both views are absolutely inaccurate. Yoga is an ancient, pagan, spiritual practice that cannot be separated from what defines it (yoga *means* to yoke, to open and unite, with the spiritual realm). And the *Yoga Sutras*—the clear, ancient, little-discussed doctrine of yoga is clearly antithetical to many religions, including Christianity.[31]

Why isn't it well known that yoga is an ancient religion? Why is it being masked as a religion-neutral philosophy in today's culture? I'll give you a guess or two.

It is no secret that changing a person's deep-rooted beliefs or opinions (such as religious convictions) is best done in baby steps. I remember learning this principle in my basic communication classes in college. The first step is to find common ground, something the person can agree with. Say, for example, something general like a platform of healthy exercise and stress reduction. Who would find anything wrong with that?

Once a mutual viewpoint is established, it becomes easier to introduce ideas that gradually move the person away from his or her previously deep-rooted position. You might call it *Persuasion 101*. I site not only my own observations of this transition. Fascinating scientific research published in the *Journal of Health Psychology* finds that while most people start yoga for exercise and stress-relief purposes, over time their purpose for maintaining the practice shifts to spiritual.

> Both students and teachers adopted yoga practice primarily for exercise and stress relief, but reported many other reasons, including flexibility, getting into shape, and depression/anxiety relief. **Over 62 percent of students and 85 percent of teachers reported having changed their primary reason for practicing** or discovering other reasons; **for both, the top changed primary reason was spirituality. Findings suggest that most initiate yoga practice for exercise and stress relief, but for many, spirituality becomes their primary reason for maintaining practice.**[32]

Interestingly, this doesn't happen when taking a step

aerobics classes. It doesn't happen with running or swimming or surfing or birdwatching or pole-jumping. Nor do we, in *any* other *non*spiritual activity, find a gradual shift in purpose from physical to spiritual. Why do you think that is?

Author and professor Candy Gunther Brown states the following:

> There's also evidence that practicing something connected with religion can actually change people's beliefs. Christians, in particular, tend to think a person's intent determines whether something is religious. They don't realize that active participation can actually change someone's intent. Over time, people who start off attracted to an alternative practice because there's a perceived health benefit start to embrace the religious ideas underneath these practices.[33]

Professor Brown is absolutely right. What is underneath the practice of yoga is what counts. And where it leads is the reason I am sharing these resources with you.

But you don't have to take my word for it. And even though she earned her PhD at Harvard and is a leading authority on the subject, you don't have to just take Professor Brown's or those who published the secular scientific study in the reputable *Journal of Health Psychology*, either. Sri K. Pattabhi Jois is known as the founder of hugely popularized Ashtanga yoga. His son, Guru Manju Pattabhi Jois, carries on the teaching of yoga throughout the world. In the quote below, Manju Jois explains his father's stance that *practice alone* is enough to reap the spiritual effects—*regardless of understanding*:

> His (Sri K. Pattabhi Jois) philosophy is that yoga would take you automatically to the meditative state, you see . . . that's how it will draw you into the spiritual path. See, that's why he says the yoga *asanas* are important—you just do. Don't talk about the philosophy—99 percent practice and 1 percent philosophy, that's what he taught. You just keep doing it, keep doing it, keep doing it, then slowly it will start opening up inside of you . . .[34]

The Jois Foundation (which changed their name to the Sonima Foundation in early 2013) advocates and makes sizeable donations to public school districts in exchange for Ashtanga yoga to be taught in public schools.[35] They also explain this view that asanas (poses) alone are a spiritual practice. While they have since washed this view from their current website as the controversy grows of propagating such a spiritual practice in public schools, dated websites have been documented expressing that asanas are the most important part of yoga because while the poses of yoga are "in appearance an external and physical discipline," they can "spontaneously... lead to the experience of the last four limbs."[36] These last four limbs are varying levels of meditation, ending in the final limb: *samadhi*, which means "union with the divine."[37]

In other words, practicing poses alone in the context of yoga can spontaneously lead the practitioner to opening and becoming one with this supreme spirit and the spiritual realm (which is the *entire point and purpose* of yoga practice) regardless of understanding or intent.

Professor Brown was invited to testify as an expert witness in the controversial Southern California case, *Sedlock vs. Baird*, which protested the teaching of Ashtanga yoga in the Encinitas Union School District. After extensive research, this was her finding on the issue:

> . . . Yoga practice—whether or not connected with verbal explanations of why one assumes bodily positions—helps one unite with the divine.[38]

YOGA FAQ

The following is a list of *frequently asked questions* about yoga, along with answers I believe you will find helpful. The coverage is not exhaustive; but it should provide some food for thought.

Q: What are the religious ideas underlying yoga?

A: Yoga is a pagan spiritual practice, and has been for thousands of years. The yogic doctrine called the *Yoga Sutras* explains the goal of all practices along this path, which is to join or be "yoked" with Ishvara, who is also called the "source of all knowledge," "ultimate consciousness," "god," or the "divine."[39] The yoga we find in studios and gyms is one of the ways to reach this goal.

Yoga means "to yoke." Many have been told it means to yoke together mind, body, and spirit. Although that sounds lovely, it is not what the term means. This yoking goes far beyond connecting the elements of one's own person. The spiritual practice of yoga is aimed at opening oneself to the spiritual world and yoking with, connecting with, and becoming one with Ishvara, the god of the practice of yoga. This god is called many different names within varying religions and traditions. "None of these pagan gods are the Lord (see pg. 135)."

Everything about the practice is designed to open the practitioner to making these connections and entering a transcendent state of spiritual awakening (i.e., of yoking with Ishvara).

(The website, www.truthbehindyoga.com, goes into further detail regarding the doctrines of yoga as they compare with the doctrines of the Bible. My opinion on the matter is quite irrelevant. But the Lord's is everything. And he makes it very clear.)

Q: Aren't we supposed to yoke ourselves to Jesus? Why don't we just do it through yoga?

A: There are two problems with this idea: First, Jesus says to take his yoke *upon* us—to walk so closely with him that we emulate everything he says and does in order to *learn from him*. He does not invite us to *become him*. In yoga, the idea is not to take a yoke *upon*, but to become "one with" Ishvara. Think about the contrasts: For Christians, taking Jesus' yoke means to walk with him, follow where he leads, and copy his example. For yoga practitioners, being yoked means to open oneself to the spiritual realm and become "one with" in the sense of *being* God by merging together as one. According to the Bible, we are not God. We never have been, nor will we ever be the Lord or any other version of a "god." The Bible clearly and adamantly repeats that the Lord is the *only* God and we are his creation. The desire to be a god has been a deception of Satan from the beginning.[40]

Consider this quote from Manju Jois: "Yoga is to unite . . . That's what *so-ham* means: I am God, I am the Creator. I am the Vishnu, the Preserver, I am the Shiva, the destroyer; and I am the Creator, the Brahma. I am all three, the three is you."[41]

So-ham is a mantra that yoga practitioners are often introduced to after they have been practicing for a period of time, typically given a vague explanation as to how it will help regulate breathing, or how it is simply a sound vibration to deepen practice. Sometimes, *so-ham* is loosely explained as meaning "I am that."[42] The meaning clearly goes much deeper.

So there's a big difference between the two! We can establish that Ishvara, the godhead of yoga, is most definitely not the God of the Bible. In Old Testament times, and in many religions to this day (including within yoga) people have worshiped gods that are not the Lord. The Bible says they are not gods at all. This is what defines them as *pagan*. This subject is further discussed in response to the next question.

In addition to yoga's goal of uniting with Ishvara, practitioners are also encouraged to deepen their experience by inviting other deities to enter or "yoke" with them to assist on the journey toward the ultimate goal of knowledge, understanding, and truth. The entire practice of yoga is movement meditation. The practitioner pays homage to and invites spirits associated with (and represented by) poses, chants (mantras), certain breathing exercises, as well as by prayers or focused intent, such as thinking about a spiritual teacher.

This is where Christians are cued to plug Jesus into yoga, along with all the other deities and energies being welcomed, to bring the practitioner peace, love, and understanding on the path to oneness with Ishvara.

Q: How do we know that *Ishvara* is not another name for the Lord of the Bible?

A: There are many ways to distinguish between the two. The Lord clearly defines who he is throughout the Bible. If this question is important to you, I encourage you to research it. On my website, *www.truthbehindyoga.com*, you will clearly see evidenced in comparative scriptures of the *Yoga Sutras* and the Bible that Ishvara is a very different character, a deity whose path and practices are forbidden by the Lord of the Bible.[43]

The God of the Bible is the Lord. He is the Father, the Son Jesus, and the Holy Spirit in one being. He declares that he is the only God, and also clearly explains that there are false gods. The Lord defines his character throughout the Bible, and he does not contradict himself. So one sure-fire way to tell that the god Ishvara is not the Lord is that Ishvara's doctrine clearly and repeatedly contradicts biblical instruction.

Here is just one example (feel free to visit the website for many more):

Ishvara's Doctrine from *Yoga Sutras* 3.25 and 3.32:
Through meditation, one can also discover spirits and communicate with master spirits.[44]

The Lord's Doctrine from Deuteronomy 18:9–12:
When you enter the land the Lord your God is giving you, do not learn to imitate the detestable ways of the nations there. Let no one be found among you who sacrifices their son or daughter in the fire, who practices divination or sorcery, interprets omens, engages in witchcraft, or casts spells, or who is a medium or spiritist or who consults the dead. Anyone who does these things is detestable to the Lord.

Q: Yikes! What does the Bible say about other deities?

A: The Bible says plenty. First and most troubling in my opinion is the Bible's position that other deities sought for assistance within yoga practice are not gods and not peaceful energies of light *at all*. God tells us clearly in many places in the Bible that behind these false gods are actually demons.[45] My own testimony evidences this truth.

The deities being sought in the practice of yoga are not the Lord of the Bible. And the divine energy (or godhead) with which practitioners become yoked is not the Lord, either. The Bible is crystal clear regarding who he is, and also about the dark truth behind any other "god."

Q: Well, can't we just plug Jesus in to our yoga practice?

A: The Lord gives his clear instruction in Deuteronomy 12:30, which admonishes us to "be careful not to be ensnared by inquiring about their gods, saying, 'How do these nations serve their gods? We will do the same.'"

Consider also, Deuteronomy 12:2–4:

> Destroy completely all the places on the high mountains, on the hills and under every spreading tree, where the nations you are dispossessing worship their gods. Break down their altars, smash their sacred stones and burn their Asherah[46] poles in the fire; cut down the idols of their gods and wipe out their names from those places. *You must not worship the LORD your God in their way.*

We are God's treasured people; we are to be sanctified and set apart for him, not copycats of those who don't know him. God calls us to separate ourselves, not to adapt and blend with pagan spiritual practices. Consider the warning from 2 Corinthians 6:14–17:

> For what do righteousness and wickedness have in common? Or what fellowship can light have with darkness? What harmony is there between Christ and Belial [Satan]? What does a believer

have in common with an unbeliever? What agreement is there between the temple of God and idols? For we are the temple of the living God. As God has said: "I will live with them and walk among them, and I will be their God, and they will be my people." Therefore "Come out from them and be separate, says the Lord."

Throughout the Bible, God gives specific instructions to ensure that his followers remain set apart. He wants us far from anything that even resembles the practices of surrounding nations that follow other gods.[47] God wants his people to be set apart, to be sanctified.

Q: Aren't you being legalistic? Aren't we free from the law as it was presented in the Old Testament?

A: You're right, we are free from the law.[48] But this is not a law issue; it's a heart issue. So, let's put aside for a moment the spiritual implications and possible effects any spiritual practice might have on us, including the research that shows that the intent of yoga practitioners changes and they become more open to the spiritual beliefs behind yoga over a period of time. And let's think about those around us.

I ask you to consider your example to others. I ask that, for a moment, you take yourself out of the equation and consider both Christians who are weaker in the faith and the non-Christians around you. I ask you to consider what your example of going to a class called yoga says to them. They know you are a Christian, so they assume the practice is "Christian Approved." Mull over those implications. Do you think your endorsement increases or decreases their likelihood of digging deeper and reading up on yogic traditions, chants, and prayers?

I assure you, those chants and prayers will be invocations of false gods. The yoga practice represents much more than exercise; those who do yoga can go much deeper without having to dig far.

Please consider the following passages:

> "I have the right to do anything," you say—but not everything is beneficial. "I have the right to do anything"—but not everything is constructive. No one should seek their own good, but the good of others (1 Corinthians 10:23-24).
> So whether you eat or drink or whatever you do, do it all for the glory of God. Do not cause anyone to stumble, whether Jews, Greeks or the church of God—even as I try to please everyone in every way. For I am not seeking my own good but the good of many, so that they may be saved (1 Corinthians 10:31-33).

Finally, I ask you to consider the Lord's instructions regarding how we should worship him with our bodies:

> Therefore, I urge you, brothers and sisters, in view of God's mercy, to offer your bodies as a living sacrifice, holy and pleasing to God—*this is your true and proper worship. Do not conform to the pattern of this world, but be transformed by the renewing of your mind.* Then you will be able to test and approve what God's will is—his good, pleasing and perfect will (Romans 12:1-3).

The Bible, for a Reason

The Lord gave us the Bible as a guidebook to communicate with him. It is a complete work. He tells us not to add to it, even if we receive revelation from an angel.[49] Everything he wants us to know about how to follow him is in the Bible. Thinking that we might know better ways to commune with the Lord than the ones he prescribes—ways that make us feel warm and fuzzy or more peaceful, or that provide some grain of "truth" that the Bible doesn't reveal—is a dangerous place to go. It is the snare that has seduced humankind from the beginning: going beyond what the Lord has clearly laid out.

In the Garden of Eden, Satan suggested to Eve that there was information beyond what the Lord had made known to the "first couple." Indeed, there was. The Lord had protected Adam and Eve from it. But Eve chose to disobey because she thought it better to discover this "truth" than to follow the

Lord's protective counsel. And she, Adam, and all of us paid for it dearly as sin entered the world.

Not much has changed since then, either in our nature or Satan's tactics. He still appeals to our pride, our desire to know more than the Lord outlines in the Bible. We're still suckers for false wisdom and knowledge, even to the point of following the pagan practices strictly forbidden by the Lord. We tell ourselves that if we do them, we will connect with him "better" or "more deeply." We think perhaps we will feel more spiritual or less stressed, or might even hope to encounter a special esoteric experience if we do it our way.

This thinking, for Christians, is a travesty. Our relationship with the Lord is not based on feelings or mysterious spiritual experiences or even seeming good health. These are actually quite easily manipulated by the other side. The Bible makes it clear time and time again that our relationship with the Lord is based strictly on faith and obedience—even if we don't agree and even when we don't understand.

The Lord allows us as Christians to represent him; he calls us ambassadors for him.[50] We have an obligation to do our best not to *mis*represent him. Whether we like it or not, our attendance at yoga classes is our stamp of approval on everything those classes embody. Most people don't know the depths of yoga's spiritual implications (many yoga *teachers* in Western culture do not even understand this). Anyone who knows you are a Christian and sees you are involved in yoga assumes the practice is fine—even for Christians. (And if people *don't* know you're a Christian, now might be a good time to search your heart and ask why that is.)

Believing you have endorsed yoga (which your participation does), they may decide to try a class. The next thing you know, they love the way it makes them feel, so they dig deeper. They try new breathing techniques and some chanting, and soon learn more about meditation and "opening" their minds.

And it all started because they thought, "We know Sally is a strong Christian, and she does it. So it must be safe." Or perhaps a young man or woman like me, who once believed in the Bible but drifted away, decides she wants to find spiritual truth. But she's not sure where to start. Should she go back to church or check out another path? She may have heard that yoga is spiritual and assumed (as many do) that *spiritual* was synonymous with *good*.

Although she knows some Bible verses about avoiding pagan practices, she's heard that yoga makes people feel peaceful, so how can that be bad? It doesn't raise any red flags because even some respected Christian women she knows talk about their yoga classes. So she assumes that yoga is a wholesome spiritual path, reasoning, "Surely, these strong Christian women wouldn't be involved if yoga was against the Bible."

So she takes a yoga class and loves the relaxing, spiritual feelings it provides her. Although chanting had always been too weird for her taste, after a while, she realizes that it's helping her become more serene. She grows to believe there is no harm in any yogic practices, and decides to read a book on yoga to learn more about the tradition.

Yet, as she digs deeper she finds more and more teachings that are contrary to the Bible. The trouble is that they are so interwoven and sugarcoated with ideas about love, joy, peace, gratitude, and gratefulness that she feels silly not believing them. At some point, she swallows the next lie—that she doesn't need Jesus to be saved. What does she need church or Jesus for? She has found a spiritual "truth" that makes her *feel* peace. But it's only a feeling. This peace is temporary. It is a lie.

This scenario is happening all over the world, and it breaks my heart. Really and truly, it ought not to be.

Yoga is not a stretch-and-tone class. *Please* understand this. It is an ancient, pagan, spiritual practice. Spirits have been associated with it and invoked by its practice for *thousands of years*. Did you know, for example, that the popular sun-salutation sequence is an act of worship to the sun god? Other poses are named after animals, celestial bodies, inanimate objects, and deities representative of pagan gods or spirits.

There are very real spirits invoked by this practice. *Period.* They are being masked in today's culture with a practice that presents itself as appealing, harmless, and even healthy. But the entire aim is to yoke the unsuspecting with the dark spiritual realm.

MEDITATION (To Think or Not to Think?)

Let me start this discussion by revisiting Ephesians 6:10–12, because it is so important to keep it in mind:

> Finally, be strong in the Lord and in his mighty power. Put on the full armor of God, so that you can take your stand against the devil's schemes. For our struggle is not against flesh and blood, but against the rulers, against the authorities, against the powers of this dark world and against the spiritual forces of evil in the heavenly realms.

God lets us know we are warring against deceptive spirits that scheme against us. He tells us elsewhere that they are so misleading that Satan, the prince of darkness, masquerades as an angel of light.[51] It is important to remember this as we seek to uncover his schemes.

Meditation is a word whose meaning has changed drastically in our culture. The 1828 edition of Webster's Dictionary defines it this way:

> **MEDITA'TION**, *noun* [Latin meditatio.] Close or continued thought; the turning or revolving of a subject in the mind; serious contemplation.

> Let the words of my mouth and the meditations of my heart be acceptable in thy sight, O Lord, my strength and my Redeemer. Psalms 19:14.[52]

Notice that Webster originally listed only one definition. It was solely connected to the biblical practice of contemplation and focused study, and Scripture was quoted to show how the word is used.

Today, popular dictionaries provide two opposing definitions of meditation: one remains rooted in the biblical tradition; another is rooted in Buddhism and Hinduism. The two are very much not the same, but they are routinely confused as such. It is important to clear up this misconception.

The Lord's instruction regarding meditation is to continually *fill the mind* with thoughts of him. Clearly, his intent is that we love him so much that we think about him always; we seek his will so ardently that we savor his Word, his instructions, and his awesome works (past, present, and future). This strengthens our relationship with the Lord and encourages us to delight in him, worshiping him with our thoughts and prayers.

This is diametrically opposed to the mindfulness/Eastern spiritual tradition, which instructs practitioners to *empty the mind* of thought, often by focusing on a single subject such as the breath, a point on the body, an inspirational person, or an object. The term *mindful* is misleading in that it does not refer to a filling of the mind, but rather speaks of a state that results from the emptying of the mind of thoughts by focused concentration without thinking about the subject of focus.

For example, if I meditate on Jesus in accordance with the biblical definition, I will think about his teachings. Perhaps I replay one of his parables and think about how it applies to my life; or I might turn my attention to and pray about a message Jesus gave that I am having a hard time understanding; or I may think about the ways Jesus shows his love to me. The point is, I am actively *thinking about* him. Contrarily, if I meditate on Jesus in accordance with the mindfulness/Eastern meditation definition, I may either picture an image of Jesus in my mind (self-induced visualization), or focus my gaze on a picture that is supposed to represent Jesus. I may concentrate on the sensation of love I feel in my heart that I believe is from Jesus. If thoughts arise, they are to be released. The point is to cultivate the state of detached mind, completely *empty of thoughts*. Do you see the difference? This is a practice aimed to let go of and clear the mind of thoughts.

We are never instructed by the Lord to empty or clear our minds with *thoughtless* focus; we are instead instructed to occupy our minds with thoughts of him, turning them over in our minds. Thought*less* focus on a subject is a very different practice than thought*ful* focus.

Some have tried to meld this biblical paradigm with the mindfulness definition of meditation that is so prevalent in our culture. They claim that biblical meditation is comparable to mantra practice (repeating a sound, word, or phrase). But hopefully the above example has begun to clarify that these are two completely different and contrary practices. Jesus even specifically warns against praying vain repetitions like those who followed other spiritual traditions.[53] His intent is for us to *think about him* and his goodness, which makes us steadfast in his ways. The pagan practice of *letting go of all thought* and emptying the mind of all thought and emotion leaves the mind wide open, with "space" to receive from the spiritual realm what feels like peace and revelations.

It is unmistakeable that these are two distinctly different definitions of meditation. They are as antithetical as the spiritual sides they represent.

The Mindfulness/Eastern Teaching

I was taught in Eastern traditions of meditation that the practice must be developed if one is to be open and able to communicate with the spiritual realm. The state of the "open mind" is a critical objective. Without it, there is no receiving from spirits. This was the first thing I was instructed to develop so that I could cultivate my communication abilities with the spiritual realm.

The practice of Eastern meditation operates under many names such as mindfulness and relaxation or stress relief techniques in an effort to appeal to a wider audience. Regardless of the name, the purpose and results remain the same. It often starts with feelings of peace, deepens to trancelike states of deep euphoria, and intensifies further as the practitioner "yokes" with whatever is invoked to create the state of openness. The peaceful feeling is not a physiological reaction to breathing or focusing. Eastern meditation is a *spiritual* practice; it produces a state of being affected by *spirit*.

Not all spirits are "good" spirits; the spirit that affects the state of being I just described is not a spirit working on the side of the Lord. *It is deception.* Its ultimate goal is for practitioners to enter a total, trancelike stillness. The purpose is *said* to be the attainment of ultimate "truth" and "enlightenment." But real truth and enlightenment are not the stock and trade of the spirits and gods with which pagan practitioners become yoked during this practice. These practitioners are as unaware as I was that they are inviting in spirits of darkness and bondage.

Just as Satan convinced Eve that the fruit would lead to real knowledge and freedom from the limitations set by the Lord, the practice of Eastern meditation promises one thing and delivers another. The professed goal is deceptive. As with anything Satan tries to use for his purposes, the real goal is to keep the practitioner from knowing the Lord, trusting him, and being saved by him. The Bible says Satan comes to kill, steal, and destroy.[54] The Eastern practice of meditation is from him.

To those of you who practice relaxation meditation techniques you may have read about in a "healthy" magazine or saw being promoted by a celebrity or popular doctor on television, this might seem like a stretch to you. But I assure you that these techniques are not only unrelated to the meditation of the Bible, they are the beginning steps on the Eastern pagan meditative path. It is my obligation to warn you that when you continue to take steps down a path, it leads somewhere; in this case to a very real, very dangerous spiritual reality masked in peace.

Satan is the master of deception. He swayed Eve by asking her whether God *really* said not to eat from the tree.[55] They both knew full well what the Lord had said: the fruit of that particular tree was forbidden. The same is true when you read in the Bible what the Lord says; you know full well where he stands on the issue. But Satan plants seeds of doubt. He makes the fruit sound or look harmless. He reassures you—*falsely*—that you will surely not die if you engage in what God forbids.

Seduced by her desire for more "knowledge," Eve took the bait. Today many of us are seduced, too; we want more "knowledge," more "peace," and some "stress-relief." Too many are taking the bait, not realizing that this practice is aimed at separating us from God.

It is important to note that the forbidden tree in the Garden of Eden was not evil. The Lord created the tree. He called it the tree of the knowledge of good and evil. There was nothing wrong with the tree. It was how Adam and Eve interacted with the tree that mattered. They went against the Lord's instructions. That was the problem.

Similarly, there is nothing inherently evil about stretching or breathing or relaxing in a cross-legged position. So where is the line? This is my advice to those of you still struggling with questions of what practices are okay and what aren't as a follower of Jesus:

If you want to pray to Jesus while you hold your push-up position, awesome—the Bible tells us to "pray without ceasing" (1 Thessalonians 5:17). Yoga doesn't get to claim exercising and stretching. And if you want to thank and praise the Lord while taking some deep breaths, do it—the Bible says to rejoice always (this includes while breathing with short *or* long breaths). God gave us breathing, and meditation doesn't get to claim it.

But here's the difference: if we continue to engage in these practices under the name of yoga or mindfulness meditation techniques, then we not only choose to defy the Lord's instruction,[56] but we potentially lead others astray by openly putting our stamp of approval on everything these practices represent. Does that make sense? It is how we approach and interact with what God has created—that is the issue.

May I suggest that the spiritual depth, peace, or stress relief we seek can be found simply by reading God's Word, fellowshipping with other believers, taking in solid biblical teaching, and spending time with him in prayer—by following *the Lord's* instructions instead of trying to "redeem" Satan's? I encourage you to try it the Lord's way, search your heart, and ask Jesus to reveal to you his heart in this matter. Perhaps getting up ten minutes earlier and pouring your heart out to the Lord in prayer and seeking him by reading a little Scripture would do wonders for the stress you aim to relieve through these meditation techniques. And instead of yoga, have you ever tried substituting the hour or so you would spend in class with simply talking to God, listening to praise music, or streaming Bible teachings through your headphones while on a brisk walk? This infuses awesomeness into my day every time. Walking is incredible exercise, and can be such a sweet, precious time for you and the Lord.

Please do not grieve the Lord by turning to pagan practices in your search for peace. The Lord loves you more than you or I can imagine, and he wants an intimate relationship with you. He wants you to turn to *him* for peace. He says in the Bible, his sweet letter to us, that he wants you and me to do this by practicing faith even when we don't agree or understand: by praying to him, reading his Word, and thinking about him and his teachings because it is good for us and will lead to life.

He never intended for us to follow a practice devised for people to commune with false gods (which the Bible makes clear are demons—see 1 Corinthians 10:19-21). When laying out his instruction for worship in Deuteronomy 12, there is a reason the Lord did not instruct his people to simply "redeem" (as many now label) the spiritual practices of those around them by plugging his name into them. On the contrary, he adamantly commanded that everything resembling the practice be burned, smashed, and destroyed. He clearly stated his intention for his people to be separate in their acts of worship, not copycats of pagans.[57] The Lord does not counsel against these methods because he is mean and wants to deprive us of peace and knowledge, but for the reason that he sees and knows more than we can wrap our minds around—he wants to keep us from death.

We have to suck up our pride in thinking that we know better, and instead trust him, because he knows best. He is the creator of all that ever was, and he loves us beyond comprehension. He won't forbid anything unless it is harmful to us. We are his people. We have to trust him and obey him. This is where true peace is found.

You may be struggling and wondering what to think about these issues. If so, I ask that you not just listen to me, but take it up with the Lord. Honestly seek his heart on the issue and ask him with sincerity what he would have you do. And look up the Scriptures; he speaks through them.

I ask for both your and the sake of others, that you follow what the Lord speaks to you. Eve's choice to disobey God's command and seek "truth" her way was not only detrimental to her. It has affected every generation in all of history. Our choices and actions also affect those around us.

> See to it that no one takes you captive through hollow and deceptive philosophy, which depends on human tradition and the basic principles of this world rather than on Christ (Colossians 2:8 NIV).

I pray the Lord continues to guide you as you seek His truth.

23
MEDITATE AND MEDITATION WORD STUDIES

The following is an extensive study of the words *meditate* and *meditation* as they appear in English in the King James Version of the Bible. These English words are translated from a variety of words in the original Hebrew and Greek, which are listed with their assigned Strong's Concordance[58] numbers and definitions. The numerals in parentheses represent the number of times each Greek or Hebrew word is translated in a particular way, according to Strong's.[59] This information amplifies the meaning by showing how a particular word is used in a variety of contexts. The idea is to gain a solid sense of the Lord's overall instruction on meditation.

For each word, I have also supplied Bible verses or passages in which the word appears. I found it interesting to compare the New International Version (NIV) renditions with those from the King James Version (KJV), so I included both for your convenience. I encourage you to look up the selections for yourself, so you can read them in their larger contexts (some added context is provided here in some cases). Understanding the context of the surrounding verses and chapters will give you a more accurate picture of the Lord's intent in using and defining these terms.

Meditate Word Study

Suwach (OT 7742): "to muse pensively"

[*Suwach* is translated: meditate (1).]

Genesis 24:63
Isaac went out to *meditate* in the field at the eventide: and he lifted up his eyes, and saw, and, behold, the camels were coming (KJV).

He went out to the field one evening to *meditate*,[60] and as he looked up, he saw camels approaching (NIV).

Hagah (OT 1897): "to murmur . . . by implication, to ponder"

[*Hagah* is translated: meditate (6), mourn (4), speak (4), imagine (2), study (2), mutter/muttered (2), roaring (1), talk (1), utter (1).]

Joshua 1:7–8

Only be thou strong and very courageous, that thou mayest observe to do according to all the law, which Moses my servant commanded thee: turn not from it to the right hand or to the left, that thou mayest prosper withersoever thou goest. This book of the law shall not depart out of thy mouth; but thou shalt *meditate* therein day and night, that thou mayest observe to do according to all that is written therein: for then thou shalt make thy way prosperous, and then thou shalt have good success (KJV).

Be strong and very courageous. Be careful to obey all the law my servant Moses gave you; do not turn from it to the right or to the left, that you may be successful wherever you go. Keep this Book of the Law always on your lips; *meditate* on it day and night, so that you may be careful to do everything written in it. Then you will be prosperous and successful (NIV).

Psalms 1:1–2

Blessed is the man that walketh not in the counsel of the ungodly, nor standeth in the way of sinners, nor sitteth in the seat of the scornful. But his delight is in the law of the LORD; and in his law doth he *meditate* day and night (KJV).

Blessed is the one who does not walk in step with the wicked or stand in the way that sinners take or sit in the company of mockers, but whose delight is in the law of the LORD, and who *meditates* on his law day and night (NIV).

Psalms 63:5–7

My soul shall be satisfied as with marrow and fatness; and my mouth shall praise thee with joyful lips: when I remember thee upon my bed, and *meditate* on thee in the night watches. Because thou hast been my help, therefore in the shadow of thy winds will I rejoice (KJV).

I will be fully satisfied as with the richest of foods; with singing lips my mouth will praise you. On my bed I remember you; I *think* of you through the watches of the night. Because you are my help, I sing in the shadow of your wings (NIV).

Psalms 77:10–12

And I said, This is my infirmity: but I will remember the years of the right hand of the most High. I will remember the works of the LORD: surely I will remember thy wonders of old. I will *meditate* also of all thy work, and talk of thy doings (KJV).

Then I thought, "To this I will appeal: the years when the Most High stretched out his right hand. I will remember the deeds of the LORD; yes, I will remember your miracles of long ago. I will *consider* all your works and meditate on all your mighty deeds" (NIV).

Psalms 143:5

I remember the days of old; I *meditate* on all thy works; I muse on the work of thy hands (KJV).

I remember the days of long ago; I meditate on all your works and consider what your hands have done (NIV).

Isaiah 33:18

Thine heart shall *meditate* terror. Where is the scribe? Where is the receiver? Where is he that counted the towers? (KJV)

In your thoughts you will *ponder* the former terror: "Where is that chief officer? Where is the one who took the revenue?

Where is the officer in charge of the towers?" (NIV)

Siyach (OT 7878): "to ponder . . . converse (with oneself, and hence, aloud) . . . utter"

[*Siyach* is translated: talk (5), meditate (5), speak (4), complain/complained (2), pray (1), commune (1), muse (1), declare (1).]

Psalms 119:11–16

Thy word have I hid in mine heart, that I might not sin against thee. Blessed art thou, O LORD: teach me thy statutes. With my lips have I declared all the judgments of thy mouth. I have rejoiced in the way of thy testimonies, as much as in all riches. I will *meditate* in thy precepts, and have respect unto thy ways. I will delight myself in thy statutes: I will not forget thy word (KJV).

I have hidden your word in my heart that I might not sin against you. Praise be to you, LORD; teach me your decrees. With my lips I recount all the laws that come from your mouth. I rejoice in following your statutes as one rejoices in great riches. I *meditate* on your precepts and consider your ways. I delight in your decrees; I will not neglect your word (NIV).

Psalms 119:21–27

Thou hast rebuked the proud that are cursed, which do err from thy commandments. Remove from me reproach and contempt; for I have kept thy testimonies. Princes also did sit and speak against me: but thy servant did *meditate* in thy statutes. Thy testimonies also are my delight and my counsellors. My soul cleaveth unto the dust: quicken thou me according to thy word. I have declared my ways, and thou heardest me: teach me thy statutes. Make me to understand the way of thy precepts: so shall I *talk* of thy wondrous works (KJV).

You rebuke the arrogant, who are accursed, those who stray from your commands. Remove from me their scorn and contempt, for I keep your statutes. Though rulers sit together and slander me, your servant will *meditate* on your decrees. Your statutes are my delight; they are my counselors. I am laid low in the dust; preserve my life according to your word. I gave an account of my ways and you answered me; teach me your decrees. Cause me to understand the way of your precepts, that I may *meditate* on your wonderful deeds (NIV).

Psalms 119:46–48
I will speak of thy testimonies also before kings, and will not be ashamed. And I will delight myself in thy commandments, which I have loved. My hands also will I lift up unto thy commandments, which I have loved; and I will *meditate* in thy statutes (KJV).

I will speak of your statutes before kings and will not be put to shame, for I delight in your commands because I love them. I reach out for your commands, which I love, that I may *meditate* on your decrees (NIV).

Psalms 119:77–78
Let thy tender mercies come unto me, that I may live: for thy law is my delight. Let the proud be ashamed; for they dealt perversely with me without a cause: but I will *meditate* in thy precepts (KJV).

Let your compassion come to me that I may live, for your law is my delight. May the arrogant be put to shame for wronging me without cause; but I will *meditate* on your precepts (NIV).

Psalms 119:146–148
I cried unto thee; save me, and I shall keep thy testimonies. I prevented the dawning of the morning, and cried: I hoped in thy word. Mine eyes prevent the night watches, that I might *meditate* in thy word (KJV).

I call out to you; save me and I will keep your statutes. I rise before dawn and cry for help; I have put my hope in your word. My eyes stay open through the watches of the night, that I may *meditate* on your promises (NIV).

Promeletao (NT 4304): "to premeditate"

[*Promeletao* is translated: meditate before (1).]

Luke 21:12–15
But before all these, they shall lay their hands on you, and persecute you, delivering you up to the synagogues, and into prisons, being brought before kings and rulers for my name's sake. And it shall turn to you for a testimony. Settle it therefore in your hearts, not to *meditate* before what ye shall answer: for I will give you a mouth and wisdom, which all your adversaries shall not be able to gainsay nor resist (KJV).

But before all this, they will seize you and persecute you. They will hand you over to synagogues and put you in prison, and you will be brought before kings and governors, and all on account of my name. And so you will bear testimony to me. But make up your mind not to *worry* beforehand how you will defend yourselves. For I will give you words and wisdom that none of your adversaries will be able to resist or contradict (NIV).

Meletao (NT 3191): "to take care of, i.e. (by implication) revolve in the mind"

[*Meletao* is translated: premeditate (1), imagine (1), meditate upon (1).]

1 Timothy 4:13–15
Till I come, give attendance to reading, to exhortation, to doctrine. Neglect not the gift that is in thee, which was given thee by prophecy, with the laying on of the hands of the presbytery. *Meditate* upon these things; give thyself wholly to them; that thy profiting may appear to all. Take heed unto thyself, and unto the doctrine; continue in them:

for in doing this thou shalt both save thyself, and them that hear thee (KJV).

Until I come, devote yourself to the public reading of Scripture, to preaching and to teaching. Do not neglect your gift, which was given you through prophecy when the body of elders laid their hands on you. Be *diligent* in these matters; give yourself wholly to them, so that everyone may see your progress. Watch your life and doctrine closely. Persevere in them, because if you do, you will save both yourself and your hearers (NIV).

Meditation Word Study

Hagiyg (OT 1901): "a murmur, i.e. complaint"

[*Hagiyg* is translated: meditation (1), musing (1).]

Psalms 5:1
Give ear to my words, O LORD, consider my *meditation* (KJV).

Listen to my words, LORD, consider my *lament* (NIV).

Higgayown (OT 1902): "a murmuring sound, i.e. a musical notation . . . a machination"

[*Higgayown* is translated: Higgaion (1), meditation (1), solemn sound (1), device (1).]

Psalms 19:14
Let the words of my mouth, and the *meditation* of my heart, be acceptable in thy sight, O LORD, my strength, and my redeemer (KJV).

May these words of my mouth and this *meditation* of my heart be pleasing in your sight, LORD, my Rock and my Redeemer (NIV).

Haguwth (OT 1900): "musing"

[*Haguwth* is translated: meditation (1).]

Psalms 49:3-4

My mouth shall speak of wisdom; and the *meditation* of my heart shall be of understanding. I will incline mine ear to a parable: I will open my dark saying upon the harp (KJV). My mouth will speak words of wisdom; the meditation of my heart will give you understanding. I will turn my ear to proverb; with the harp I will expound my riddle (NIV).

Siyach (OT 7879): "a contemplation; by implication, an utterance"

[*Siyach* is translated: complaint (9), lament, meditation (1), prayer (1), talking (1), communication (1), babbling (1).]

Psalms 104:33-34

I will sing unto the LORD as long as I live: I will sing praise to my God while I have my being. My *meditation* of him shall be sweet: I will be glad in the LORD (KJV).

I will sing to the LORD all my life; I will sing praise to my God as long as I live. May my *meditation* be pleasing to him, as I rejoice in the LORD (NIV).

Siychah (OT 7881): "reflection . . . devotion"

[*Siychah* is translated: meditation (2), prayer (1).]

Psalms 119:97-99

O how love I thy law! it is my *meditation* all the day. Thou through thy commandments hast made me wiser than mine enemies: for they are ever with me. I have more understanding than all my teachers: for thy testimonies are my *meditation* (KJV).

Oh, how I love your law! I *meditate* on it all day long. Your commands are always with me and make me wiser than my enemies. I have more insight than all my teachers, for I *meditate* on your statutes (NIV).

NOTES

[1] Hebrews 9:27.

[2] An ashram is a place of spiritual study and retreat, typically of Hindu and Yogic traditions.

[3] *Yoga Sutras*, 1.25. http://www.ashtangayoga.info/source-texts/yoga-sutra-patanjali/chapter-1/ (accessed March 18, 2015).

[4] *Yoga Sutras*, 1.27. http://www.ashtangayoga.info/source-texts/yoga-sutra-patanjali/chapter-1/ (accessed March 18, 2015). *Please be aware that many watered-down versions of the *Yoga Sutras* exist. I reference the traditional, more accurate, literal translations rather than the modern, popularized translations that mask true meaning and the reality of the practice.

[5] *Yoga Sutras*, 1.28–29. http://www.ashtangayoga.info/source-texts/yoga-sutra-patanjali/chapter-1/ (accessed March 18, 2015).

[6] 1 John 4:8, 16.

[7] Job 9:3–4 NIV.

[8] See Luke 22:42.

[9] See Chapter 21.

[10] For the sake of clarification: energies, deities, and spirits are all essentially the same thing, and I use the terms interchangeably.

[11] Alanna Kaivalya and Arjuna van der Kooij, *Myths of the Asanas: The Stories at the Heart of the Yoga Tradition* (San Rafael, CA: Mandala Publishing, 2010), p. 16.

[12] One more thing: Besides Satan's appearance in the well-known story about Adam and Eve in Genesis chapter 3, the Bible also talks about the serpent in Revelation, the last book in the Bible. Revelation 12:9 describes what is going to happen in the future: "And the great dragon was hurled down, that ancient serpent, who is called the devil, or Satan, who leads the whole world astray. He was hurled to the earth, and his angels with him." So there's that to think about.

[13] See Mark 5; Luke 8.

[14] 2 Corinthians 1:21. (Please note that here and elsewhere, not

every applicable Bible passage is listed. There are many more, and I encourage those who are interested to do further personal study.)

15 2 Corinthians 11:14.

16 See Matthew 4:10; Exodus 20:3; Deuteronomy 5:6–7.

17 See Revelation 22:8–9; Colossians 2:18.

18 See Hebrews 4:14–16, Ephesians 2:18. Matthew 24:36 clearly shows that the angels are not all-knowing. We are to pray only to the all-knowing, all-powerful God. Hebrews 2:5 explains that the world to come has not been subjected to angels, but to the Lord only. Hebrews 1:4–8 draws the contrast between the angels' position and role, and God's.

19 John 8:44. See also Revelation 12:9; 2 Corinthians 11:14.

20 See Psalms 22:3 KJV.

21 See 2 Corinthians 5:17.

22 Lee Strobel, *The Case for Christ: A Journalist's Personal Investigation of the Evidence for Jesus* (Grand Rapids, MI: Zondervan Publishing House, 2013).

23 There are many places where this teaching is exemplified. The following is not an exhaustive list: Mark 10:52; Mark 5:34; Luke 17:19; Luke 8:48; Matthew 9:22; Luke 7:50; Luke 18:42.

24 See Matthew 10:32–33; John 3:18; 2 Corinthians 1:22.

25 John 14:6.

26 See Ephesians 2:8.

27 See Ephesians 2:8.

28 See Hebrews 10:25.

29 See Romans 12:4–5.

30 See Hebrews 11:6.

31 See http://www.truthbehindyoga.com/what-the-bible-says1.html and http://www.ashtangayoga.info/source-texts/yoga-sutra-patanjali/ (accessed March 18, 2015).

32 Crystal L. Park, Kristen E. Riley, Elena Bedesin, and V. Michelle Stewart, "Why Practice Yoga? Practitioners' Motivation for Adopting

and Maintaining Yoga Practice," *Journal of Health Psychology* (July 4, 2014): 1-10. Boldface added by author.

[33] Ruth Moon, "What Christians Need to Know about Alternative Medicine," *Christianity Today*, October 22, 2013, www.christianitytoday.com/ct/2013/november/nonchristian-roots-alternative-medicine-candy-gunther-brown.html (accessed December 27, 2014).

[34] Guy Donahaye and Eddie Stern, *Guriji: A Portrait of Sri K. Pattabhi Through the Eyes of His Students* (New York: North Point Press, 2010), 7.

[35] http://www.utsandiego.com/news/2013/jul/31/yoga-encinitas-grant-teachers/; http://www.nclplaw.org/wp-content/uploads/2011/12/Sedlock-Yoga-Oral-Argument-Press-Release-2-13-15-FINAL.pdf. (accessed March 30, 2015).

[36] http://web.archive.org/web/20120818140147/http://www.joisyoga.com/about-ashtanga-yoga.html#parampara (accessed March 19, 2015). Emphasis author's own.

[37] http://www.expressionsofspirit.com/yoga/eight-limbs.htm (accessed March 19, 2015).

[38] Candy Gunther Brown, "Declaration of Candy Gunther Brown," *Motion for the Issuance of an Alternative Writ of Mandamus; Memorandum of Points and Authorities; Declarations of Jennifer Sedlock, Candy Gunther Brown, Ph.D., and Dean R. Broyles, Esq.* Note 45, http://www.nclplaw.org/wp-content/uploads/2011/12/DECLARATION-OF-CANDY-BROWN-FINAL.pdf (accessed January 21, 2015).

[39] International Info Page for Ashtanga Yoga, See verses 1.24-1.27 http://www.ashtangayoga.info/source-texts/yoga-sutra-patanjali/chapter-1/ (accessed March 18, 2015).

[40] See Isaiah 14:12-14; Genesis 3:4.

[41] David Kelman, "Interview with a Guru: Prodigal Son," *FIT Yoga*, August 2005, p. 81. http://www.kripalu.org/pdfs/manju_jois_article.pdf (accessed January 22, 2015).

[42] http://en.wikipedia.org/wiki/Soham_%28Sanskrit%29 (accessed March 30, 2015).

[43] www.truthbehindyoga.com (accessed March 30, 2015).

Notes

44 http://www.ashtangayoga.info/source-texts/yoga-sutra-patanjali/ chapter-3/ (accessed March 18, 2015).

45 See Deuteronomy 32:17; Leviticus 17:7 (NKJV); Psalms 106:37; 1 Corinthians 10:20; Ephesians 6:10–12.

46 *Asherah* is the name of a pagan, false goddess that was worshiped in Old Testament times.

47 Jon Courson, *Jon Courson's Application Commentary: Old Testament Volume 1: Genesis–Job* (Nashville: Thomas Nelson, 2005), 420 (s.v., "Leviticus 19:28").

48 See Romans 8:1–2.

49 See Galatians 1:6–12.

50 2 Corinthians 5:18–20.

51 See 2 Corinthians 11:14.

52 *American Dictionary of the English Language, Webster's Dictionary 1828—Online Edition*, s.v. "meditation," http://webstersdictionary1828.com/ (accessed January 17, 2015).

53 See Matthew 6:7.

54 See John 10:10.

55 See Genesis 3:1.

56 See Deuteronomy 12; www.truthbehindyoga.com (accessed March 30, 2015).

57 See Deuteronomy 12.

58 All definitions of the listed Hebrew and Greek words are from Biblesoft's New Exhaustive Strong's Numbers and Concordance with Expanded Greek-Hebrew Dictionary, CD-ROM, Biblesoft, Inc. and International Bible Translators, Inc. (1994, 2003, 2006).

59 This data summarization was gleaned from *Blue Letter Bible*, www.blueletterbible.org (accessed January 17, 2015).

60 "The meaning of the Hebrew word for this is uncertain," according to the *Life Application Study Bible* (Carol Stream, IL: Tyndale House Publishers, 1988), s.v. "Genesis 24:63."